MR. MOONLIGHT OF THE SOUTH SEAS

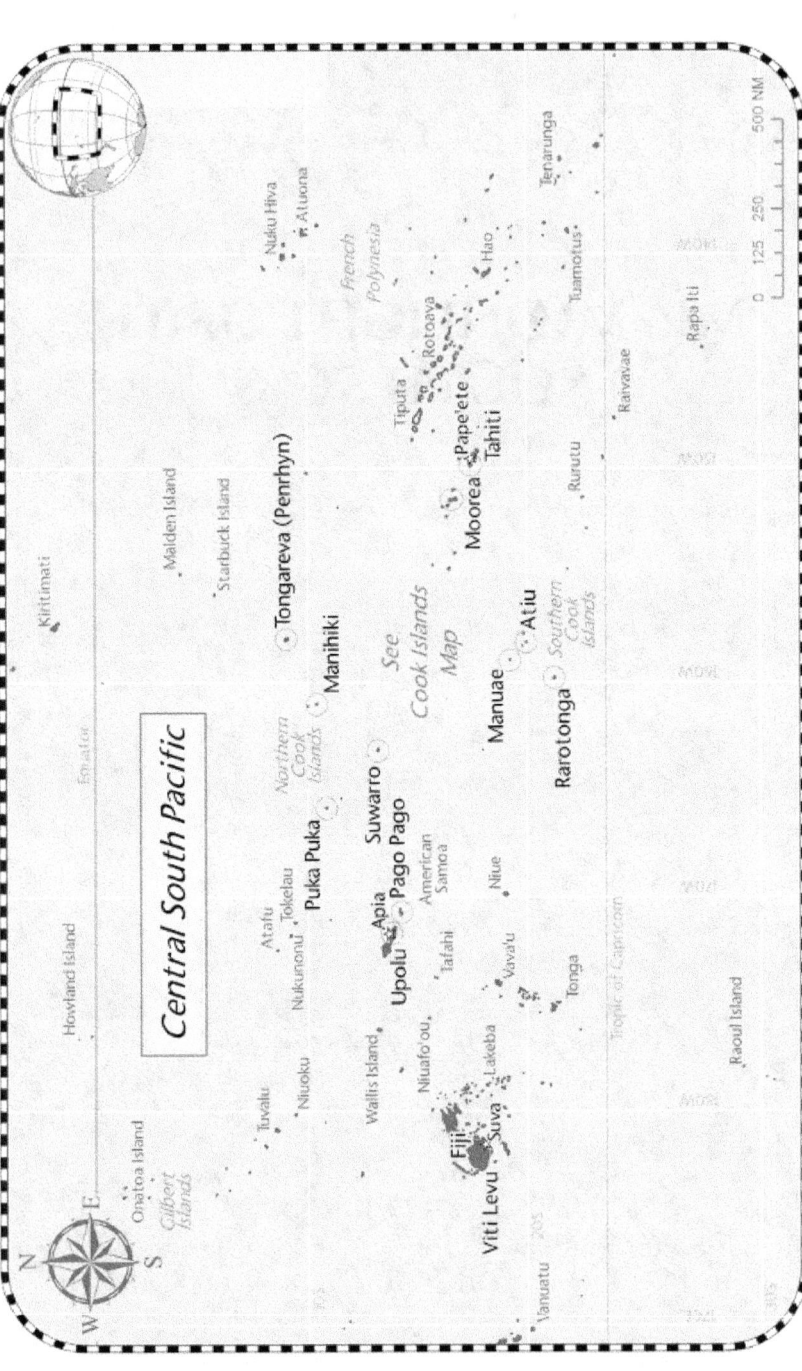

MR. MOONLIGHT OF THE SOUTH SEAS
THE EXTRAORDINARY LIFE OF ROBERT DEAN FRISBIE

BRANDON OSWALD

Mr. Moonlight of the South Seas
Second Edition

Copyright © 2022 Brandon Oswald

All rights reserved. No part of this book may be reproduced in any form without permission in writing from the publisher, except by a reviewer who wishes to quote brief passages in connection with the review published in printed or electronic media. For permission requests, please address Publish Authority.

Published 2022, by Publish Authority
300 Colonial Center Parkway, Suite 100
Roswell, GA 30076-4892 USA
PublishAuthority.com

Editor: Bob Laning
Cover design: Raeghan Rebstock

ISBN 978-1-954000-08-7 (Paperback)
ISBN 978-1-954000-09-4 (eBook)

Originally published 2017 by Dockside Sailing Press and is reprinted by permission of DSP and the author.

Printed in the United States of America

For my parents

PREFACE

My association with Brandon Oswald began in 2002 when he, and other volunteers from the United States, were on the island of Rarotonga in the Cook Islands to assist local education and health services. Brandon and I formed a productive partnership. My work at the Cook Islands Library and Museum was supported by his expertise as an archivist. For my part, I was happy to share my knowledge of what it had been like in this part of the world and to review Brandon's manuscript; particularly as it pertained to my father, the writer Robert Dean Frisbie, and his close contemporaries James Norman Hall and Charles Nordoff.

Thank you, Brandon, for your continuing friendship and interest in our family.

Florence (Johnny) Frisbie
Honolulu, 2017

CHAPTER ONE

THE BEACHCOMBER FROM CLEVELAND

In 1996 a small group known as the Robert Dean Frisbie Society gathered at a grave in a tiny corner of a cemetery on the island of Rarotonga, Cook Islands. They were there to commemorate the centennial birth of American author, Robert Dean Frisbie. It was not a well-documented ceremony that possessed a huge fanfare and was full of pageantry and fireworks. In fact, most avid readers to this day have never heard of him, or the significant contribution he made towards Pacific Islands' literature. When I stumbled upon an article that was written by Lisa Williams for the *Pacific Island Monthly* and titled, "Celebrating a Famous Son," I was hoping that she would expound on the day's festivities in honoring a very unique author. Unfortunately, her short piece did not capture the ceremony, but instead it focused more on his life. One paragraph, however, caught my attention because I believe it summed up the essence of Frisbie:

> Those who don't see his books given prominence in local libraries are missing out on the warmth and unique insight Frisbie passed on through his work, as well as his contributions through being a keen observer of island life and culture and a serious student of island history, traditional canoe building, fishing and celestial navigation.

Today his six books are out of print and difficult to find. One may have luck finding the books on Amazon.com or at an Internet book trading shop. But be forewarned, the interested reader will most likely have to break his piggy bank to afford one of the titles. Frisbie also wrote over two-dozen articles for various magazines throughout his lifetime. Some of these can be found on the Internet, but sadly many of them seemed to have faded away and disappeared. This is a real shame as his writings were molded by his life perhaps more so than any other South Seas author. In 1944 the young American author, James A. Michener, met Frisbie in Samoa and stated that Frisbie was "the most graceful, poetic and sensitive writer ever to have reported on the islands."

I can recall that one of the first South Seas publications that I bought was Frisbie's, *The Book of Puka-Puka*. The odd title fascinated me because I liked the way it poetically sounded whenever I pronounced it. When friends and family came to my house and saw the book sitting out, the title would inevitably catch their attention usually causing them to giggle at the word, "Puka-Puka." They had no idea that Puka-Puka was an actual place. Without a doubt it would be the book that I would read over-and-over in every room of the house. The spine of my copy was worn to the point where I had to keep it together with rubber bands. Eventually, I would glue it together, and then glue it again. It was like a person's favorite shirt that was hard to throw away even after years of wear and tear.

I believe that the opening sentence in the special introduction of the *Book of Puka-Puka* that was written by A. Grove Day truly captured the essence of Frisbie and his work throughout his life. Day wrote, "His greatest dream in life was to write a book like Herman Melville's *Moby Dick*, which would tell the absolute, unveiled truth about one man's thoughts and feelings." To find this truth it may take weeks, months and years, and I think this was where Frisbie was a bit more unique than many of his contemporary South Seas writers. As most writers who wrote about the South Seas visited the islands and then returned home, Frisbie went and stayed. Because he stayed, he eventually found the truth in thoughts and feelings through his daily adventures and experiences. Sadly, his chosen island lifestyle would also take its toll emotionally and physically, as well as it became a financial burden on him and his family. The *Book of Puka-Puka* would be his first publication to show this, and the one that many avid readers of the genre, like me, would never forget.

Frisbie's story does not begin in a warm part of the United States or on a tropical island, rather it began in the Great Lakes region of Cleveland, Ohio where he was born on April 17, 1896 to parents Arthur Grazly Frisbie and Florence Benson from Vermont. Over the years some have called the city The Big Plum and the Mistake by the Lake. Call the city what you will, it certainly is not the place where a South Seas writer would likely come from. When I discovered this, it intrigued me. I am not sure why. Maybe it was because I have close ties with the city. Although I am a native Californian, my parents are from Cleveland and moved west in the 1960s. During my pre and early teen years in the 1980s they used to send me to Cleveland where I bounced around from relative to relative throughout the summer months. They believed that this was the best way for me to spend time with relatives who lived far away. I enjoyed the visits. It certainly beat going off to some kids' camp during the summer. My relatives always treated me like that lost nephew or cousin who had found his way home.

Cleveland was wonderfully strange to me. It was simply a world apart from Southern California. It was verdant, industrious and had (still has) some of the most rabid sports fans on earth. The homes were charming and cozy and yards were open. I never saw a fenced in yard. It had bizarre animals like groundhogs and chipmunks. I loved playing kick-the-can with my cousins until midnight and going to ethnic restaurants with my aunts and uncles where they told me horrifying stories about winter. Does it really snow here? On hot and humid nights, while waiting for songs from *Asia* and *Duran Duran* to be played on the radio, I tried to imagine the place under twelve-foot snowdrifts and picking snowball fights with my cousins. Today whenever I stargaze on a balmy night in some South Pacific Island, I often think back to my time in Cleveland. Even the pesky mosquitos helped bring back wonderful memories.

The Cleveland that Robert Dean Frisbie was born into was a far different place than the one that I visited in the early 1980s. In 1896 the city was celebrating its centennial and the Cleveland Chamber of Commerce believed that this was a momentous event, and the city deserved to commemorate the advancements it had made in population, wealth, commerce, education and arts. They chose a five-person committee whose job it was to stage such a jubilee. A three-month celebration from July to September was planned that began with a salute from the Cleveland Light Artillery at midnight on Founder's Day, July 22nd. Other events during the summer months included parades, a yacht regatta, a floral exhibition, a Women's and Early Settler's Day and the illumination of the Centennial Arch that spanned Superior Avenue and looked very much like the *Arc du Triumph* in Paris. The celebrations ended on September 10th with Commodore Perry's Victory Day when the city hosted spectacular entertainment on the lakefront including a "Battle of Lake Erie" reenactment.

Not much was recorded about Frisbie's first few years except that he was a thin, frail, and sickly boy who devoted his life to his mother. He was a voracious reader and read everything he could get his hands on, especially enjoying the works of Herman Melville and Robert Louis Stevenson. Frisbie would later admit that since his childhood he had always liked to reach the end of things. For example, he often found a curious fascination in walking to the farthest point of a promontory, in climbing to the top of a mountain, or exploring the headwaters of a river. In 1908 when Frisbie was twelve, his family was recorded as moving to California. When I read this, I couldn't help but wonder if Frisbie thought that California was as strange to him as I had felt about Ohio.

Although Frisbie's father was born a Quaker, he sought comfort and assistance in other religions such as the Theosophists, the Christian Scientists and the Order of the Magi. This incessant search would also force the family to move from place to place. American author, James Norman

Hall, one of Frisbie's closest friends throughout his life, heard a forlorn account about Frisbie's father and their early life in California. Frisbie described his father to Hall as a gentle, kindly man, but without depth of character or a will of his own.

All his life his father had searched for a religious faith to join. Frisbie told Hall that his father looked for new religions among the cranks and frauds who made a business of supplying "faiths" for profit. Because of this, the family went from one sect to another, forcing Frisbie to attend the kind of private school that was set up for these sects. The family eventually ended up in Southern California where Frisbie's father joined the Theosophical and alternative commune in Point Loma (San Diego), California known as Lomaland. Frisbie states, "It was heaven for my father, a dozen varieties of heaven, but it was hell for me."

Lomaland was established and overseen by Katherine Tingley in 1897. She intended to establish a community that would model the philosophical and humanitarian goals of Theosophy. This doctrine taught about God and the world based on mystical insight that followed mainly Buddhist and Brahmanic theories. She felt a profound sympathy for the victims of poverty, misery, and war and worked all her life to alleviate suffering. She believed that no matter how depraved a person had become or how severely physically, emotionally, and spiritually handicapped, human beings still had an unlimited capacity for improvement. Tingley began living at Lomaland in 1899 and built a worship structure called the Temple of Peace (or Aryan Temple) as well as a residential facility known as the Homestead. Lomaland became a regional center for the arts under her energetic leadership.

Census figures indicated that from a population of 95 in 1900, the community grew to 357 in 1910 and declined only slightly in 1920 to 320. At its height in the 1910s, 500 adults and children lived in the community.

In the summer of 1900, the educational arm of Lomaland called the Raja Yoga Academy ("Raja Yoga" meant divine union) opened with five students. At the age of 12, their father placed Frisbie and his brother Charles in the school. The educational goals of the school involved not only the intellectual formation, but it also involved moral and spiritual development as well. By 1910 the school boasted an enrollment of 300 students. It is hard to imagine that the precocious and withdrawn Frisbie would overachieve at this school. Some observers criticized that the Raja Yoga's atmosphere was repressive. Discipline was military: strict and swift. Children wore uniforms, marched to classes and saluted their teachers. They sat rigidly upright during classes and meals. They maintained silence at all times except for necessary conversation. Tingley believed that silence nurtured the soul. Another controversial aspect of the school was that children lived apart from their parents in homes known as "Lotus Houses."

One might think that since the academic curriculum was balanced, it might have appealed to Frisbie. Although classroom instruction was given to the usual subjects of the era like grammar, mathematics, science and modern languages, there was emphasis on literature, poetry and art. These are subjects at which Frisbie would have excelled. Additionally, students did calisthenics, worked in the community garden and learned music and drama. Tingley wanted to establish a student-centered school rather than a teacher-centered one, encouraging independence of spirit in her students. Music was taught formally and students learned an instrument at a very early age. In fact, some students learned to play an instrument before they knew how to talk. It was not surprising that the school had a full orchestra and several choirs.

Unfortunately, this strait-laced religious school isolated students from the sinful world and taught the tenets of a pseudo-mystic religion. Frisbie later stated that students were told that the Grimm Fairy Tales, Santa Claus and orthodox spooks did not exist and that no literature on such topics was allowed in school. This could be damaging to one so creative. Frisbie eventually amassed an extensive library of books. When he first sighted the island of Pukapuka, he thought of his long search for an island where he could be a law to himself and enjoy the five or six hundred books that were boxed up in the ship's hold. He could read what he wanted and when he wanted with very little distractions.

According to Florence Johnny Frisbie (Frisbie's eldest daughter) Frisbie lasted about four years at the Raja Yoga Academy—a lot longer than one studying the author would have guessed. She noted in an introduction to one of her own books that Frisbie and his brother slept on pillow-less beds, arose at six o'clock seven days a week and followed this by vigorous military drill before breakfast, which was eaten in silence. Religion was never taught to the children. Frisbie had been in almost constant rebellion at the school as he tried to run away twice and also tried to burn down one of the houses.

The end of Lomaland came gradually, but inevitably, as donors passed away and expenses began to soar, the community was in debt. In 1929 Tingley died suddenly and unexpectedly from injuries sustained in a car crash. The stock market crashing certainly did not help things and was another devastating blow to the community. Nevertheless, Lomaland hung on until 1941 when the property was foreclosed and was then moved to Covina near Los Angeles. Since 2001 the Point Loma Nazerene University has occupied the land where Lomaland once stood and continues many of the best of Point Loma Theosophist traditions: education with a spiritual bent and emphasis on ancient religious wisdom. It also continues to be a big advocate of fine arts and theater in the San Diego region.

I tried contacting the organizations that may contain records for the Raja Yoga School and anything regarding Robert Dean Frisbie. I learned that records could be in one of three places. These include the Theosophical Society based in Altadena, California, Blavatskyhouse in the Netherlands and

the Alexandria West Special Collections in Turlock, California. I contacted all three places regarding any information on Frisbie. Sadly, each one only sent me a letter telling me to try to contact the other place. I kept running in circles like a dog chasing his tail. This was a real shame because I was hoping that some kind of information would unveil new insights about Frisbie.

Ironically, for the past few summers my daughter attended a violin camp at the Point Loma Nazerene University. For the first couple of summers, I had no idea that Frisbie attended school on this same campus. But when I started doing research on him, I couldn't believe that he once lived in the same county that I do now and that he went to school where my daughter goes to camp. During the next camp I started to pay a little more attention to the buildings and the environment of the Point Loma Nazerene University. It became more than just a "drop off" and "pick up" place for my daughter. I found that a few of the buildings are still in existence from the time that Frisbie attended the school. This

included the Greek Amphitheater where many dramas and orchestra concerts were staged.

I also heard that one of the Lotus Houses was still in existence and I was determined to find it. So, one afternoon before picking up my daughter, I set out to discover this house. I first asked a gardener who just pointed in a direction. I don't think that he really understood what I was trying to ask him, but away I went. I remember that it was a beautiful warm day as the sun glistened off the azure water of the Pacific Ocean. Believe it or not this kind of weather is a rarity for this time of year when the marine layer and fog usually darken the area like a spooky coastal location of a horror movie. I eventually found the building and tried to go inside, but the door I wanted to open was locked. I tried opening it again with a little more muscle. It was definitely locked. I thought about tracking down someone who could help. I looked around for an employee of the college, but saw no one. I wasn't feeling especially proactive to find anyone to help me, so I gave up.

And like a laid-back Californian, I just stood there and admired it for a short spell.

After a reflective few minutes staring at the building, I decided to walk over to the Greek Amphitheater which was a just a short distance from the Lotus House. When I got there, I sat down on the block of the last row of the back and stared at the stage area. I wondered what, if any, productions Frisbie might have been involved with on this stage. I doubt the stories of Frisbie's favorite authors, Melville and Stevenson, were ever staged. Then I started to daydream about a stage production of *Moby Dick*. That amused me. I guess it could be done. The worlds that they are creating on stage these days can be quite mind-blowing. Melville would probably turn in his grave but he wouldn't be the first author to do that. Besides, I have seen worse kinds of stage productions in my time. Then a group of co-eds, summer school students sat down in the theater not too far from me. Their giggling, eating and texting on their phones broke my daydream. I then realized that I was late picking-up my daughter and quickly walked towards the music building.

My daughter was waiting for me on a curb swinging her violin case impatiently to and fro. I wasn't that late. As I approached her from a different direction than usual, she looked at me quizzically. "Where were you?" She couldn't help but ask.

"Just chasing my white whale," I answered. She looked out towards the ocean, as I put on my sunglasses. I really didn't know what I was talking about. But I was feeling cool and poetic. I grabbed her violin case and we headed home.

By 1917 the Great War was raging in Europe. It was a stalemate with no end in sight. It was a war of attrition. Peace talks stalled and went nowhere. Although the United States wanted to remain out of the conflict and clung to the idea of isolationism, the Allies needed help. They needed it badly and knew if the Americans entered the war with its vast resources of men and materials, the tide could definitely be turned. All the Germans had to do was leave the shipping lanes alone with their submarines, but they didn't. They sunk merchant ship after merchant ship killing innocent Amer-icans. The gloves finally came off and President Wilson went before a joint session of Congress to request a declaration of war against Germany. On April 4, 1917, the U.S. Senate voted in support of the measure to declare war on Germany. The House followed up with their support two days later. It was the turning point of the war. The end was nigh. Finally.

Frisbie was twenty-one years old in 1917 and eventually enlisted in the United States Army toward the end of the war. In 1918 he was in the 8th Cavalry training camp in Texas. Although he became Editor-in-Chief of the Texas Army newspaper called Saber, he did not enjoy his time in the military, despite wanting to do his bit for the war cause. James Norman Hall, who was also a World War I veteran, noted that Frisbie hated army life and was not cut out for a regimented existence. Perhaps it was too much like his Raja Yoga School days. Hall stated, "His lungs have always been weak and camp life did nothing to improve the condition. He would have been invalided out of the service had the war not ended when it did." At Frisbie's last medical examination in the Army, the doctor reportedly told him that he would not be able to live out another winter in America. Hall reports that the doctor told Frisbie that unless he was extremely careful, his prospect was that of a bed in a tuberculosis sanatorium. Frisbie was medically discharged with a monthly pension of $45.00 a month. It would be an amount that in his later years made a difference between mere existence and near-starvation for him and his family on a South Seas atoll.

I tried writing to the National Personnel Records Center (Military Personnel Records) to see if I could get any additional information regarding his army and medical history. I knew that retrieving any medical information would be a long shot since I'm not related to him, but it was worth an attempt since it only cost me the price of a stamp. After several weeks of waiting, I walked my dog to the mailbox and was surprised to see a letter addressed to me from the National Personnel Records Center. I eagerly opened it at my mailbox like a desperate reporter in dire need of a story, hoping to discover some tantalizing scoop about Frisbie that nobody else knew.

I quickly moved to the light of the dim streetlight. I thought, "What good are those things?" I dramatically struggled to open the letter and then squinted to read it even without my glasses. This is how it happens in the movies! But, alas, the juicy information that nobody else would know about wasn't meant to be. It was just a simple letter stating that my request had gone unfulfilled and that the information that I was seeking was not in their files. Apparently on July 12, 1973 parts of the archives suffered a fire and most of the files were destroyed. As an archivist myself, I knew that there was not much an archivist can do to recover files after a fire. I admit that I was disappointed. It is frustrating when your research hits a dead end. Although I have received my fair share of rejection letters over the years for various endeavors, I wasn't going to lose any sleep over this small setback. I quickly shrugged off the disappointment. There were going to be plenty of other research opportunities ahead of me.

About a year later, Johnny sent me a group of photographs of her father at various stages of his life. A few of these interested me because they were ones that I hadn't seen before on the Internet. The one that caught my eye most of all was a photo taken in Marfa, Texas during the First World War of him dressed in a military uniform. Out of the thousand words that this picture held, sickness was definitely not one of them. He looked young and fit and was shown holding an object. The object was not one that a person would expect to see in such a picture because it wasn't a rifle, or a sword or a flag; it was a wind instrument. In fact, it was a clarinet. Johnny mentioned that he played in the army band, and I wondered if his musical talents stemmed from his time at the Raja Yoga School. The picture also showed how proud he was to be offering his service to his country and no doubt that the news of his discharge was disappointing to him. Thirty or so years later he would get another chance at helping his country during the Second World War, which would take place on most of the islands around him.

Caption: Robert D. Frisbie in Uniform

To Frisbie the news of possible death if he did not change his environment felt like the end of the world to him. He fought sickness all his life including tuberculosis (TB), which ran rampant in the United States during the late 19th and early 20th century. It would cause more deaths in industrialized countries than any other disease during this time. All cases of TB are passed from person to person via the air. When a person infected with active TB coughs, sneezes or spits, they release the TB bacillus that can be inhaled by another person. This is why it was such a horrible disease in the industrialized world where so many people lived in close proximity. It reached across all classes in the 19th century.

Although TB would continue to wreak havoc to people of the lower classes and became more closely linked to those in poverty, by 1900 better nutrition, housing, and sanitation in wealthier classes reduced their risk for contracting the disease. It was often called consumption and typically starts in the lungs causing chest pain and severe coughing, but can spread to other organs including the kidneys, spine and brain. Infected people coughed up sputum and often blood. They had fevers, night sweats, chills and weight loss.

Tuberculosis was known as the romantic disease. In the 19th century those who suffered from the disease had an aura of exceptionality that made them standout in the eyes of their contemporaries. TB was seen as the inevitable result of a life dedicated to a lavish or unique lifestyle and was not in accordance with socially common behaviors, routine activities, and established morals. How often have we seen the disease exhibited in art? It had certainly become an important theme in literature, music, and film. Puccini's opera, *La Boheme*, comes to mind right away. The death of Mimi is an unforgettable moment. The protagonist in Eugene O'Neill's Pulitzer Prize winning play, *A Long Day's Journey into Night*, suffers from consumption. In the introduction to the publication, *The Cruise of the Janet Nichol* Roslyn Jolly posed the question why Fanny Osborne was so attracted to the eccentric, often sickly young writer, Robert Louis Stevenson. She states that Fanny was attracted to Stevenson because of the flavor of Bohemia that surrounded him and behind it the solid value of access to high culture that Louis promised. There is also a long list of other authors that created characters with TB such as Dostoevsky, Hugo, McCourt, Remarque, and Sinclair, just to name a few. Movie actors such as Ingrid Bergman in *The Bells of St. Mary*, Val Kilmer in *Tombstone*, and Nicole Kidman in *Moulin Rouge* met their sad, unforgettable demise at the hands of the disease. Even Jimmie Rodgers and Van Morrison constructed songs about TB. Ironically, Rodgers would eventually pass away from the disease.

The process of demystifying TB and its "romantic" image began in the 20th century. As TB began to lose its expression of morbid elegance, the healthcare profession invested heavily in public health policies to combat the disease. A person with TB was not looked at as a bored dandy or an enchanting courtesan anymore. Rather, the ordinary man who suffered from the disease was perceived to be someone who lacked resources and lived in an industrialized urban center. TB became the shameful disease that did not have a cure and was associated with hunger, the incapacity for one to provide for one's family, and excess. Alcohol and partying vigorously were the most mentioned excesses that revealed reckless and immoral behavior and were considered the way one contracted the disease.

There is a reason why I bring up the morbid topic of TB. Not only did the disease spoil Frisbie's young life, it would also provide a major and unexpected turning point in his later years. One frustrating symptom of the disease was that a high percentage of people who got infected with TB developed a latent TB infection where the bacteria were alive in the body but inactive. People who have latent infections do not have TB symptoms and cannot spread the disease to others. However, if left untreated, the TB bacillus can become active and be symptomatically and contagiously problematic. In other words, the disease can lie dormant in an individual. If and when the immune system weakens like Frisbie's did, the odds of the disease to reinvigorate itself becomes greater.

After his medical discharge from the United States Army, Frisbie took the physician's recommendation of a "complete climate change" to heart. Johnny Frisbie noted that her father's desire to leave America became an obsession. He cared little about his friends and lost all interest in advancing his education. Frisbie held various but mostly journalist and columnist positions for newspapers. He worked as a reporter for the *Army's Marfa* in Texas, and then made his way to Fresno, California where he wrote for the *Morning Republican*. Sometime after April 1920 Frisbie decided to suddenly leave America to become a "South Seas beachcomber." He wrote in the opening pages of his novel, *My Tahiti*.

 An island attracts one strangely and inexplicably. In our youngest days few pleasures have been so great as exploring some tiny bank formed by forking streams, or of dreaming that some day we shall sail to an island in the...moonlight solitudes mild of the mid-most ocean....

The South Seas sirens were calling and Frisbie was answering. He was not the first literary figure to answer the call and definitely will not be the last.

CHAPTER TWO
SOUTH SEAS SIRENS

Tom Richards, a trader in the South Seas during the early 20th Century, nails the "call of the sirens" motive when he wrote:

> The Hula girls came out. They danced with vim and vigor, ogling men in the hope they would take them for car rides later. They got a-top tables and the movements of their bodies made men's eyes light with a lustful fire, and the blood rise to their heads and pound in their temples. The music. The night, the crowd, the charm of Tahiti and these girls carried them away.

A man once told Richards that Tahiti is the Kingdom of the Devil himself and that he challenges any man to resist the influence of this place. We can trace back to the diaries, notes, and stories told by Captain James Cook and his crew, or

William Bligh and his mutinous bunch of ragamuffins how South Seas maidens were the most desired above all else that the region can offer. The South Seas woman was often described as beautiful, barely dressed, and easy to be acquainted with. How many men jumped ship for them? How many sailors did they lure to their demise? Richards admitted that island life and the intimate touch with colored and unsophisticated people had made a sharp division in his moral code and that the white man who seduces a colored woman is rarely troubled with pangs of conscience.

Women were not the only sirens to attract men to the South Seas. Frisbie noted that the free and easy life enticed the insatiable lechers, the alcoholics, and the businessmen. There were the deluded beachcombers that he described as a "hungry set of men." The islands also attracted the Don Quixotes such as high school boys with their guitars and their heart on their sleeves. Many men came to the South Seas to simply be alone on a beautiful island. Frisbie found these men fascinating as many of them came to futilely escape from business worries, from ill-health, from wives and families, from prohibition, and some came to escape from themselves. Most of them returned home after a few months or moved on. Some died, for the climate is conducive to injudicious drinking and fornication.

In 2002 I took my first trip to the South Seas volunteering on the island of Rarotonga, Cook Islands by signing-up with the nonprofit organization, Global Volunteers. It was a nearly month-long trip where the majority of the twenty-or-so membered team came to the island to help teach children reading at various schools around the island. A few members who had a background in the medical field were assisting at the hospital. I was different as I came to help with libraries. Who would've thought that on this little speck of an island that was only about twenty miles in circumference and had an area of twenty-six square miles, that there would be more than one library? Indeed, there were several different kinds of libraries throughout the island that were found at schools, in town, and at colleges. Little did I know at the time that this trip would eventually serve as an inspiration for me to create my own nonprofit organization dedicated to providing archival assistance to cultural heritage organizations such as archives, libraries, and museums throughout Melanesia, Micronesia and Polynesia.

Although I worked in various libraries throughout Rarotonga, it definitely wasn't the books or the library profession that drew me there. The sirens that called me to the South Seas were the literary writers who wrote about the area and excited my imagination. I was always captivated by the way Frisbie and his contemporaries described the Pacific Islands and the way that their characters lived a carefree, beachcombing lifestyle that one can only find in such a place. If there was one thing that all the South Seas writers had in common it was the way they made you feel that you were on a tropical island. They excelled at allowing the reader to smell the frangipani flower, taste crabmeat soaked in coconut milk, see the different shades of blue in a lagoon, or feel the coolness of a stream in the middle of a steamy jungle. Their stories were dreamy, romantic and adventurous and placed you in front of an exotic, untamed backdrop. I can recall reading my first South Seas tale, *Mutiny on the Bounty*, by James Norman Hall and Charles Nordhoff and being swept away by the three distinct adventures that were caused because the crew of the *Bounty* simply didn't want to leave the idyllic island of Tahiti.

Brandon Oswald at Muri Beach, Rarotonga

During long breaks from work, I would bike over to Muri beach. Here I would take a quick dip in the lagoon followed by a rest on the beach to gaze at the *motus* in the near distance and thought about beachcombing. I'd have the whole beach to myself. What a life. One could never starve here with all the friendly islanders and the fruits and vegetables growing wild throughout the island. And I love fruit, especially island fruit. Mangoes, bananas, paw-paws (papaya) and star fruit grew in abundance. I imagined an island girl dancing to the rhythm of a drum and the beat of the breakers crashing upon the lagoon. I'd swing my guitar around in front of my salt-crested chest and begin strumming a ballad while another island girl sitting on her knees listens attentively to each word. Oh, what a life. This is the place for me. Sadly, inevitably, my fantasy ended abruptly as a family of five rudely crashed with their towels, snorkeling gear and beach accessories not more than five feet from me. They had the entire beach and they had to pick a spot that close to me? With my daydream disrespectfully distracted, it was a good time to leave.

In the late 19th century, while maritime, whaling, and missionary frontiers had lost their vim and vigor, the literary one remained important. The lure of paradise in literature emerged as a constant foil and escape from increasing commercialization and industrialization, especially in America. Writers such as Herman Melville in the 1840s were at the forefront of literary figures writing about the South Seas. Melville, born in 1819 in New York, had financial difficulties and supported himself since he was in his teens. A young adventurer by heart he was eventually lured to the Pacific in 1840 by the whaling frontier that was then in its heyday. He signed on the whaling vessel, *Acushnet*, which was headed to the South Seas. Over the next four years Melville lived the sailor-beachcomber life and deserted his ship at the island of Nuku Hiva in the Marquesas. This experience became the basis of his book, *Typee*, subsequently followed by its sequel, Omoo. With these two books, Melville drew on the travelogue tradition to produce an incredible portrait of the life on a Pacific Island. His adventures and description of the beautiful, remote island caught the imagination of many writers and non-writers at home. And let's not forget about one other thing too, sex! Who can forget the desirable, luscious love interest, Fayaway, in *Typee*, or the beautiful, yet incorrigible Sadie Thompson in W. Somerset Maugham's *Rain*? The old adage "Sex Sells," was never truer for the sales of a South Seas novel.

Around the same time Richard Henry Dana wrote his book, *Two Years Before the Mast,* which pictured his life at sea and on the eastern Pacific coast and that also captured the fancy of future South Seas writers. From this point on, writer after writer departed for the Pacific using the books and novels of their predecessors as guide and inspiration. In 1866 Mark Twain, who was then a young reporter for the *Sacramento Union,* took passage to Honolulu. He was mostly interested in observing the whaling and missionary era and to write a series of letters for a paper that would claim future commercial opportunities for California businessmen in Hawaii. However, like Melville, Twain felt compelled to write about the effects of western civilization on the Polynesians. After four months, he sailed home but never forgot about Hawaii. The most important literature about his time in Hawaii was written in his book, *Roughing It,* which was published in 1872. Although his reports on the islands were not as sexy as, say, Melville's, he did approach them in the anecdotal style of the gold-rush tradition. It was an adventure told by a true adventurer.

Following the path of Melville, Dana and Twain, Robert Louis Stevenson was the next literary great to venture out to the South Seas. In 1888 Stevenson, accompanied by his wife, Fanny, stepson and even his mother, set sail to many islands including the Marquesas, Tahiti and Hawaii. He expected that his South Seas cruise would heal him emotionally and physically, and he wanted to find a place that would cure his tuberculosis. He wrote to a friend stating, "I have found a yacht, and we're going the full pitch for seven months. If I cannot get my health back...'tis madness; but of course, there is hope, and I will play big." Stevenson would remain in the Pacific Islands until his death in 1894.

After visiting most of the island groups in the South Seas, Stevenson settled in Samoa. There he would go on to write several acclaimed Pacific short stories such as "The Beach at Falesa," and "The Bottle Imp." He also wrote the novella *The Ebb-Tide*, which was published in 1894. He detailed his three cruises and adventures in letters he wrote to his friends, exulting in his newfound health. He also wrote about the incidents of life on the open sea and captured the fascinating life and cultures that were far away from anywhere else in the world. Although he enjoyed the physical beauty of the islands, his major literary themes were human degeneration and the debilitating effects on Polynesians that stemmed from contact with Western civilization. These themes were very similar to the ones that Twain was trying to bring to the attention of his readers. But Stevenson, perhaps, went even further. He studied South Seas politics in hopes to adopt plans that he believed would ensure harmony between the whites and the indigenous races of the region. His 1896 publication, *In the South Seas*, (published posthumously) was written from material that he collected from his three cruises. It revealed a shrewd observer of human nature and politics and viewed the islanders as humans who were not without a valid culture of their own.

The thirty-one year old Jack London set sail from San Francisco on April 23, 1907. His wife, Charmain, was one of the five inexperienced sailors that accompanied him on the journey aboard his sailing vessel, *Snark*. The crew first sailed to Hawaii that was now part of the United States. London was the first major American author to experience Hawaii as an American territory rather than as a royal kingdom. He delved into the island's history, customs and psychology for his short stories, but he longed for more. Although Hawaii was an exotic escape from the mainland America at the turn of the century, he felt that the full literary frontier was not restricted to that island. Hawaii was already too Americanized. He wanted to find more inspiration deeper in the South Seas. Following his muses, Melville and Stevenson, he sailed the *Snark* to such places as: Tahiti, Samoa, the Marquesas, and the Solomon Islands. *The Cruise of the Snark* recounted his adventures and hardships of his two-year voyage and was published

in 1911. It became a bestseller and remains one of London's most popular works.

Ideally London had intended to reprise Joshua Slocums's circumnavigation of the globe. Unfortunately, his trip to the South Seas was cut unexpectedly short because London and his crew began to contract various island illnesses such as malaria, yaws, tropical ulcers and even severe sunburns. Eventually his hands and feet swelled so much that he could not perform duties aboard the ship. He had no choice but to sail to Australia and find a way back home to California. Although he was severely disappointed, he regretted nothing as he and his crew experienced the hospitality of the Pacific Islanders. They were often greeted with feasts, celebrations and lavish expressions of goodwill. London and his crew were also avid photographers that produced around four thousand photographs during the *Snark* voyage. Many of these photographs can be viewed at the Huntington Library in San Marino, California and at the Jack London State Historic Park in Glen Ellen, also in the same state. London would continue to write stories about the South Seas after his adventurous cruise. Like other writers in the 19th century, the themes of Jack London's stories ranged from paradise reminiscences to tales of debauchery and decline.

W. Somerset Maugham was an English novelist, playwright and short-story writer who also qualified as a surgeon at St. Thomas Hospital in London. During World War I he volunteered with the Red Cross and the American Volunteer Motor Ambulance Corps The patients he saw while in medical school were nothing like the horrors of war he saw on the front line and, he wrote in his diary, "I have never seen such wounds." In 1915, Maugham left the front because he was recruited by the British Secret Service to begin work in Switzerland as a member of a network of British agents who operated against the Berlin Committee.

To the surprise of many colleagues, friends and family, Maugham abruptly left Europe in 1916 and headed to the South Seas during, what seemed to be, the middle of the war. The reason for his leaving was to continue his role as a secret agent. He was sent to Samoa to acquire relevant information about Germany and its use of the island's powerful radio station, the threat of its military forces and the danger of its warships cruising the Pacific Ocean. He stayed for several months before moving on to another island. Maugham was always fond of traveling because he believed it provided relief from the strain of writing and to refresh his mind.

By early 1917, Maugham made his way to Tahiti. He utilized this trip as a research expedition for one of his most popular South Seas novels, *The Moon and Sixpence*, published in 1919, which was based on the life of artist Paul Gauguin who lived on the island from 1895 until his death in 1903. He spent weeks interviewing people who knew the eccentric and gifted painter. Maugham was especially interested and motivated by Gauguin's Bohemian lifestyle and his fascinating departure from the mundane life in the city. He was also drawn to and admired Gauguin's desire to embrace a primitive existence while leaving behind the constraints of ordinary society.

Maugham's pragmatic view of the world would be found in many of his short story works regarding the South Seas. Unlike the romanticized accounts of some of his predecessors, such as Herman Melville and Robert Louis Stevenson, Maugham saw the Pacific as a place where gloomy, depraved European men became trapped in an inescapable environment that burdened them emotionally and physically and by their relationships with the islanders. His short story *Rain*, published in 1921, told the story of a clash between a missionary and a prostitute while the missionary was stranded in Pago Pago, Samoa. This work remains a prime example of Maugham's dark and desperate themes. The story's popularity has sustained over the years; it has been adapted for the stage and filmed on three separate occasions. Maugham once wrote about the Pacific region, "The Pacific is inconstant and uncertain like the soul of man." In his opinion, the islands possessed a rich heritage of folklore and myth, much of which was being overshadowed by colonialism. Although the South Seas writers who came after Maugham would personally witness his opinion, they would also endeavor to optimistically rekindle the romance and old customs of the islanders.

By 1920 the pioneering work of these literary greats continued to attract new writers to the South Seas. Two of

Frisbie's contemporaries and good friends, James Norman Hall and Charles Nordhoff, were American World War I veterans who decided to move to the Pacific Islands and settled in Tahiti. The Great War seemed to create an even greater need to find relief from the stress and destruction of the modern world, especially for veterans who were also writers. When Hall returned to his quaint, simple hometown in Iowa from Europe, he noticed the vast changes in the spirit of American life that was moving forward too fast and felt uneasy about the changing times. For example, he despised the automobile that he felt was speeding up the tempo of life. Tahiti on the other hand was more to his liking. It was slow-paced and charming. As a writer, Hall shared the same philosophy and was influenced by essayist and critic, Edmund Wilson. Wilson believed that writers in the 1920s should take refuge from the "perplexities and oppressions" about them by "retreating into a fantasy land" which was usually an idealization of a contemporary region remote from the centers of power or of a bygone era.

Like Hall, Nordhoff (who was from California) hated change as well. The two friends agreed to meet in California before heading to Tahiti. They both set sail for Tahiti in January 1920 and settled in their new island home quite quickly. Hall admits to a period of "loafing and observing" in order to get a feel for the daily life and customs of the people of Tahiti. Both young men loved to make frequent fishing trips with native boys or excursions into the valleys. They both married Tahitian women. Nordhoff married within the first year that he was there, and Hall's nuptials took place in 1925. In a letter to his mother shortly after arriving in Tahiti, Nordhoff wrote, "These islands are certainly ideal for the man in search of a little peace—no affectation, no prying, no hypocrisy, no worry."

As for work, they agreed on writing travel articles for a friend of theirs who was an editor at *Harper's Magazine*. It was not until 1932 when the young collaborators published their first South Seas book titled *Mutiny on the Bounty*. Nordhoff hits the nail on the head again when he wrote, "The atmosphere of the South Pacific which I am beginning to feel already is a strange one: beauty almost too great to be endurable; beauty which brings a vague heart-ache, a haunting sadness impossible to define." These themes were used throughout many of their novels. *Mutiny on the Bounty* was quickly followed by two other novels titled, *Men Against the Sea* and *Pitcairn's Island*, and were subsequently published by 1934. Collectively the three novels would be known as the *Bounty Trilogy*. These novels had it all—drama, adventure, romance, and mystery—that took place in front of an enchanting, yet dangerous and exciting backdrop. With these books, Hall and Nordhoff achieved a wide audience. Hollywood came calling and transferred their most famous book to film in 1935 starring Charles Laughton as Captain Bligh and Clark Gable as Fletcher Christian. Future collaborations on books would lead the pair to a lucrative literary career. Some of these endeavors were also turned into movies. These included *The Hurricane, The Tuttles of Tahiti* (based on the novel *No More Gas*), *High Barbaree* and *Botany Bay*.

In late 1920 James Norman Hall spotted the tall, gangly Frisbie disembarking from the steamer ship that came from San Francisco in the port town of Papeete. Like many South Seas ports, Papeete was teeming with activity as traders, sailors, natives, fisherman and beachcombers did what they did best before the afternoon siesta. Tahitian girls were dancing to the songs of a string band and welcoming the newcomers to their beautiful island. This practice still exists today. How often have we seen the images of Hawaiian girls placing leis around the necks of the newly arrived tourist?

Every South Seas nation has its formal way of welcoming people into their island. I can recall that when I first visited Rarotonga, Jake Numanga and his ukulele serenaded my fellow Air New Zealand passengers and myself. Jake was a Cook Islands national icon. He performed every day for every arriving flight and has done this for over thirty years. He starts playing when the first person enters the airport from the tarmac and doesn't stop until the last person leaves with their luggage. After a long flight, it was nice and welcoming. As I stood in the customs line, my sleepy body awoke to his lively crooning and reminded me that I was in the part of the world where love, respect and living in harmony was truly practiced.

In the 1920s, Papeete, Tahiti was the place. If it was happening in Papeete, it was happening in the Pacific. The island was the starting point for those seeking adventure. This was the island that Captain James Cook visited, mapped its coastline and oversaw the collecting of specimen. He also recorded the rare celestial event known as the transit of Venus in 1769. The island's beauty and the pretty, promiscuous women were two of the reasons why Christian Fletcher led a group of mutineers against Captain Bligh twenty years later. Nordhoff described the island quite eloquently in a letter to his mother:

 The island is beautiful with an unearthly loveliness impossible to describe—its strangely jagged skyline against the dawn; its encircling lagoon, bordered with a ring of white where the surf breaks on the reef; its rich and varied vegetation. The mountains inaccessible and never visited, run up to 7000 feet, and are bordered by a ring of flat land two to four miles wide. Cocoanuts, avocados, mangos, bananas, coffee, vanilla, limes, oranges, sugar cane, yam, beans, swarms of wild chickens—all these things make life easy for the man who has a few acres of land. Dozens of streams rush down from the interior—cold pure water, so soft that soap is scarcely necessary.

After Captain Cook brought back to England thousands of illustrations of Tahitian flora and fauna as well as the first map of the islands of the Pacific, interest and knowledge of Tahiti and the region began to grow among Europeans. In the 1800s the arrival of whalers, British missionaries and French military expeditions changed the way of life on Tahiti forever. The island became a tug-of-war for control between the British and the French. The Pomare Dynasty ruled Tahiti until 1847 when Queen Pomare finally accepted French protection of the islands of Tahiti and Moorea. France recognized the sovereignty of the Tahitian state. The Queen would be responsible for internal affairs, while France would deal with foreign relations and assure the defense of the island.

In 1880 following the queen's death, King Pomare V, who had little interest with the affairs of the kingdom, was persuaded rather easily to cede Tahiti and most of its dependencies to France. By 1903 the French Establishments in Oceania was created which collected together Tahiti, the

Society Islands, the Austral Islands, the Marquesas Islands and the Tuamotu Archipelago. All of these islands would eventually be reconstituted as the overseas French territory called French Polynesia in 1957.

Frisbie as a Young Man

Frisbie would later write about his wanderings throughout Papeete. He wrote that the strangeness of the place delighted him and that he finally felt that he was breaking into a land of adventure that was forbidden to all save a fortunate few. He saw old-fashioned carriages, shays, surreys, spring wagons, filled with natives from the country districts. The women all but lost in innumerable folds of calico and fathoms of ribbon, and great hats with ruffles, streamers, and plaited affairs. The men were stiff and self-conscious in their tightly fitting black coats and white trousers. In some of the shops Frisbie could hear the accordion playing like that of side-streets in Paris. In open doorways he saw natives lounging about bottle-littered tables and Tahitian girls dancing. He felt that these scenes were unreal and belonged in the volumes of Stevenson and Melville.

But on the day of his arrival, Frisbie did not notice the hustle and bustle of Papeete. Hall noted that Frisbie held a portable typewriter in one hand and a camera in the other. Their friendship that would last until Frisbie's death almost thirty years later began instantly as Hall pointed out to him how pretty the street bordering the waterfront looked in the morning light. Frisbie did not notice. He was too self-absorbed with his South Seas dreams, and responded quite reverently, "It's what I hoped it would be as a jumping-off place. All these ships... ...I suppose you can go almost anywhere from here?"

The two new friends walked along the waterfront where Frisbie became fascinated with every type of boat from copra schooners to fishing cutters. Hall quickly realized that Frisbie wanted to buy a boat most of all. It was Frisbie's dream and the boat would be his home for the rest of his life. He explained to Hall that he planned to bring the boat with him wherever he went like a hermit crab carrying his shell. "I read somewhere that there are thirty thousand islands in the Pacific. Do you suppose that's true? Not that I expect to visit all of them; only the loneliest ones." Perhaps it is every writer's dream to find that place of heavenly solitude to write the masterpiece. Hall understood. They would spend the rest of the day together talking mostly about Frisbie's dreams and the plans that went along with them.Like many artists before him, Frisbie stayed at the Hotel Tiare for a spell. He loved his solitude but also enjoyed companionship. Besides artists, the hotel attracted all sorts of colorful, South Seas characters like traders, sailors, natives and beachcombers. It did not take long for Frisbie to make friends. He especially found conversations interesting when talking with schooner captains who entertained him with their stories of storms at sea, pearl diving, and drinking. In one of his books, *My Tahiti*, Frisbie wrote about the verandah of the Hotel Tiare stating, "...that there may be many hotel verandahs where one can drink Cointreau, breathe deeply the scent of exotic flowers, listen to finer music; but the geniuses of such places are less romantic spirits than he who haunted the Hotel Tiare. And in other places, I fancy, men are less susceptible to the little sentimentalities of life. In Tahiti, from the traders to the frankly sensuous natives, little attempt is made at restraint."

Hall would often meet his American friend and have long and serious conversations. He would describe Frisbie as a dreamer who had something of a child's gift for make-believe. Hall quickly learned about another personal dream that Frisbie had, which was to write something great that would become his "Moby Dick." This great work would be completed within twenty-five years and solitude would be crucial. Therefore, Frisbie believed that he must be alone with himself most of the time. It was a dream that would obsess him for the rest of his life. Hall was impressed with the nonconformist and was quite sympathetic with Frisbie who had chosen the difficult and unpredictable career of a writer. "I don't care how long it takes me," he enthusiastically told Hall. "I will work for years, all my life if necessary, to write my one book. I can live on my pension until I have it finished. But in the end, I hope I can make a name for myself in my one small field."

Hall was mostly silent, watching the ambitious new writer churn his plan over and over within his mind. Frisbie feeling a bit anxious asked, "Do you think I'm an idiot? It may be true. I've had no education except what I have picked up for myself by reading.

I dream of writing this great book and I can't even spell properly, to say nothing of writing the King's English."

Hall finally broke his silence by asking, "If it means so much to you, why not try it? If you failed, would that be such a tragedy?"

"To me, it would."

"I don't see why," Hall replied. "You might find the result quite otherwise. You might be led off on another track toward something you could do really well." Hall could tell that Frisbie lacked a bit of confidence and that he truly worried about his self-doubt. But Frisbie had his dream, and the South Seas love to make or break a man's dream. Being sensible and pragmatic are virtues needed to survive in these harsh, yet indulging lonely dots of land in the vast Pacific Ocean.

For the next four years, Frisbie settled down to island life never forgetting his dreams. He built himself a small bamboo and palm-frond thatch house in Papeari, about thirty-five miles from the town of Papeete. He enjoyed his solitude for writing and the escape from noises of village celebrations. But this is Tahiti after all, with plenty of food, drink, Tahitian women and fascinating customs that he would write about in the near future. Thus, it was quite difficult for him to completely ignore these celebrations. As he wrote in *My Tahiti*, "A man enjoys his solitude only if he can enjoy people too. One adds zest to the other."

The more Frisbie saw of the Tahitian's free, uninhibited manner of living, the more he respected their culture. Above all, Frisbie truly admired their lack of hypocrisy in their personal and social relations and believed that losing this is the heavy price the Tahitians paid for becoming "civilized." He also thought their lack of moral restraints was noteworthy, yet to be emulated. His daughter, Johnny, wrote that her father lived with a Tahitian girl named Terii for a few years. In a letter to his mother Frisbie tells her not to be shocked that he is not married but living with a woman. "There are no marriage ceremonies down here," he told his mother. "When a man and a woman fall in love, they just consider that their love is sufficient without a piece of paper and a priest's benediction." Of course, this was a bit of an exaggeration, as he truly wanted the Tahitians to hold on to their unrestricted, fancy-free lifestyle from the everyday presence of missionaries and the government of France. Frisbie would definitely change his tune after meeting the love of his life in Pukapuka.

Frisbie made many acquaintances during these first few years on the island and learned the language quite quickly. The Tahitians liked Frisbie and he liked them. They began calling him Ropati, which was a phonetic approximation of

"Robert." He would eventually be known throughout the islands as Ropati of the South Seas. Through these newfound friends, Frisbie learned how to fish and pearl dive. He also became accustomed to the flora and fauna of the island that were very similar all over the Pacific Islands. He dabbled in being a plantation owner and spent many happy days paddling his outrigger canoe along the lagoon that bordered his side of the island. A neighbor even offered to teach him navigation, which he eagerly accepted and learned the traditional ways of charting the stars.

In 1921 Frisbie rebuilt a thirty-foot yawl with the help of two friends named E.J. Spies and R. A. Sampson. They called the boat, *Motuovini*. Because of a lack of funding, the renovation of the boat in the village of Papeari would take over two years to complete. Once the boat was ready, they planned on exploring the numerous uncharted, or rarely visited islands and reefs near the equator. If one of these islands was well liked, they planned to establish a kingdom of their own and make laws to suit themselves like boys playing in a tree house. To prepare for the long trip at sea. Frisbie developed an even deeper understanding of navigation by the many books that his mother and brother had sent him.

Problems fell upon the adventurers from the beginning. Shortly before they were to set sail, a grippe (influenza) epidemic hit the island. When an epidemic hits an island, it hits hard as there are usually not many places to run, hide and wait it out. It was thought that the illness was brought to the island by a boat from New Zealand. Another setback happened when Frisbie stepped on a poisonous rockfish, or *onu*, while he was fishing. The poison from this fish is known to kill people and Frisbie became quite scared of his own mortality during the couple of weeks that he was laid up. He even wrote to his mother stating, "I seem to realize the material significance of it too clearly and I fear the end of my ego, my personality, which I unluckily love." Also, during this time his girlfriend, Terii, left him to marry a Tahitian boy.

After recovery from these misfortunes, they were ready to sail again until the island received a wireless warning of a giant tidal wave moving towards Tahiti. This created an intense excitement causing a bit of a panic throughout the island. Fortunately, when the wave hit the island it was only eighteen inches high which relieved the islanders who managed to muster a nervous laugh about it. Finally, the *Motuovini* was able to set sail much to the joy of the sailors. The three men sang songs and drank rum and danced to the rhythm of drums during their farewell party.

The adventurers made quite an impressive journey with their yawl. They sailed their way through uninhabited smaller islands of the Society Islands, as well as the Cook Islands. One of their more memorable stops was on the island of Manihiki in the northern part of the Cook Islands where they received a huge reception from the natives. Manihiki was a coral atoll consisting of forty tiny islets that were encircled by a lagoon two and a half miles wide. The atoll was best recognized for its pearl farming especially the cultivation of the special black-lipped mollusk known as the *Pinctada Margaritifera* or black-lip mother-of-pearl. Manihiki was also known for having the most beautiful women on earth which Frisbie and his fellow sailors would never ignore. Apparently, at the time of their arrival the *Motuovini* was the second "overseas boat" to ever put into the island during the lifetime of its inhabitants. According to the *Pacific Age* in Suva, Fiji, it was reported that "a great reception from the natives who all assembled on the beach near the vessel, bringing presents of flowers, mats, etc., and performing dances for the edification of the plucky navigators." And in true Pacific Islands' fashion, a feast followed shortly after their arrival and the revelry lasted through the night.

After Manihiki, the *Motuovini* continued its amazing journey throughout the South Seas. They visited Tongareva and Suwarrow in the Cooks as well as American and British Samoa. In September 1923, the end came quite suddenly for the small crew in Suva, Fiji. Since the trio could not live in Fiji without money to last them through the hurricane season, they were forced to sell the boat for £300 to enable them to make their way back to Tahiti. This must have been devastating to Frisbie as he was very proud of his little boat and the remarkable adventure it gave him. He wrote to his brother, Charles, saying, "It is a sad thing to part with a friend and that is how I feel about the *Motuovini*. The little ship is proud now, for she has sailed three thousand miles over the high seas and rode majestically through one ninety-mile gale." Despite the disappointing end of his journey, the experience that he gained on this adventure would be used as fodder for many of his writing endeavors for years to come.

Hall noted that Frisbie seemed to be giving a lukewarm attempt at his ambitious project of writing the great novel. Perhaps, Hall thought, Frisbie realized that he was too young to attempt it at the time and that more experience at learning the culture of the region was needed. Other sources pointed to the contrary. Frisbie stayed busy writing especially during long breaks that took place with the construction of the *Motuovini*. According to Johnny, her father collaborated with

Hall on a handbook on the Polynesian language and wrote a novel titled, *Tingley Book*, but discarded it because he felt it was too morbid. Additionally, during his time in Tahiti, Frisbie joined with two other literary-minded men to form the "South Seas News and Pictorial Syndicate." They covered news of all the islands in the Society group. The staff consisted of Charles Brown, who was a successful writer for *Adventure* magazine, as president, and Charles H. Norris as business manager. Frisbie was the managing editor. Business was moderately good, mostly because they had no competition.

In her book, The *Frisbies of the South Seas,* Johnny wrote that during her father's time in Tahiti, he prolifically finished articles for American publications. She mentioned that the *San Francisco Chronicle* published a few of his articles such as "When the Black Death Shook Papeete," "Will Politics Save the Polynesian Race," and "An E Flat South Sea Island King." The *Fresno Republican* published "Last Cannibal Now Mormon Missionary," and "Aspiring Young Men May Now Become Kings." She states that he even wrote two ghastly tales for the *Saturday Evening Post* titled, "The Maneared Serpent of Lake Vaihere," and "The Phantom Canoe of Moorea." Unfortunately, The Post believed that these two stories were a bit "weird," for there are no records of their publications. I scoured the Internet for these titles, especially the ones supposedly published by the *San Francisco Chronicle* and the *Fresno Republican*, but had no success. Maybe I was just being cheap because I didn't want to pay for an online membership that I would hardly use, if at all, in the future. My research budget was very limited. Some online newspaper subscriptions can cost and there is nothing worse than paying for a subscription and ending up finding nothing.

Upon arriving in Tahiti after his adventure in the *Motuovini*, Frisbie learned that a publisher accepted an article that he wrote. It was titled, "Fei-Hunting in Polynesia," and was published by *Forum* magazine in 1924. This was the first-known publishing success for Frisbie. Fei is a plantain that grows in the jagged cliffs of Tahiti. The article was, perhaps, Frisbie's experience of going on a *fei* hunting expedition with one of his neighbors, Tuahu, who had adopted him as a son by Polynesian standards. The story was about a white man (*popaa*) proving himself that he is a true son of the islands as Frisbie had to carry a heavy load of fei (nearly two hundred pounds) from the treacherous cliffs of Autara back down to the village. After much struggle and help from his foster father, he made it to the village with his bundle of *fei* much to the chagrin of the villagers who believed that he would crumble under the heavy weight. Although Tuahu carried most of the weight for Frisbie, he was never prouder of his adopted son. Whenever he was asked about his Frisbie, he boastfully said, "He is like one of the ancient race, this son of mine—a true child of the islands. He carries five large bunches at a time, passing the young men who rest along the way and not stopping once till he reaches the sea." This kind of success was what made a legend in the islands and brought hard-earned respect from the scrutinizing people of a village.

But something was not sitting right with Frisbie upon his return to Tahiti. After such an energetic adventure that was full of excitement, merriment and horror, it was hard for him to accept the landlubber way of life. The publication of *Fei Hunting in Polynesia* gave him a little boost in confidence which was something that all writers craved for at one time of their career. He began to think more seriously about his writing career and wanted to go to a place where he could concentrate on developing himself as a true writer. He wrote to his brother Charles and said, "I am going to settle down to five years of solid work. My work will be writing. If at the end of this time it appears that I will ever be able to do anything better than mediocre work, then I will continue. If not, then I am free to quit and lead a life of ease."

Frisbie left Tahiti in early March 1924 and sailed about seven hundred miles southwest to Rarotonga, the capital of the Cook Islands group. On this island the A.B. Donald Trading Company was interested in Frisbie's mother-of-pearl discovery and experience the year before. This was when he had visited the islands of Manihiki and Penrhyn. They wanted to send him there to man a trading station. This suited Frisbie very well as he had hoped to return to Penrhyn and experiment with cultured pearls, as well as he wanted to continue his writing. This could be the exact island that he was looking for. According to Johnny there was another reason why he wanted to go back to Penrhyn. It was another siren by the name of Teanua.

Unfortunately, life on the island was not what Frisbie had hoped it would be. He could not find the solitude that he wanted more than ever. He also grew less and less enchanted with Teanua as the love affair was not as steamy as when they first met during his visit to the island on the *Motuovini*. Frisbie's island girl kept leaving him for a native boy every time he ignored her to work on his writings. He also felt that Teanua would not be able to adjust to his life of increasing isolation. He decided to leave the island and took an offer from the A. B. Donald Trading Company to operate a long-forgotten trading post on another isolated island in the Cook group known as

Pukapuka. Little did he know that this change, and his eventual toils, observations, adventures, frustrations, and romances on this far-flung island would create a unique and introspective writing style that would add his name to the specialized list of immortalized South Seas writers.

CHAPTER THREE
DANGER ISLAND

Alexander Bell Donald and his partner Charles Edenborough started a cargo business in the late 1870s and over the next thirty years the firm bought about fifteen ships for trades from Auckland to Rarotonga, Samoa and Tahiti. At its peak, all inward cargo had to be picked and loaded to reach the Auckland markets. Although the ships' decks had great appeal with high piles of sweet-smelling tropical fruit, a storm or contrary winds could make the difference between profit and disaster. Donald himself was unwilling to leave the timing to the judgment of others during bad storms and often travelled on his vessels, supervising the buying and selling. In the mid-1890s Donald assumed complete ownership of the business when Edenborough retired.

The firm was then incorporated in 1896 as A. B. Donald Ltd. Donald passed away in 1922 and left the business to be carried on by his five sons. One anecdotal story (that would make an art collector and even the unsophisticated art fan cringe) comes from the company when in late 1890s there was once a struggling artist who needed to travel from Papeete to one of the outer islands in the Marquesas group. He had no money and no means to pay his passage so he offered the Master of the A. B. Donald vessel some of his paintings. During the voyage the Master was unimpressed with the paintings, deciding that they were rubbish and threw them overboard. The artist was Paul Gauguin, the French post-impressionist artist who moved to Tahiti in 1891 with the desire of escaping the constrictions of European society. Like other artists before him, he hoped that the South Seas would provide a personal and creative freedom and outlet to pursue his art.

By the time Frisbie came to the South Seas, the A.B. Donald Company used many ships for its trading business. The *Tagua, Avarua, Vaitere,* and the *Tiare Taporo* were a few of the popular ships owned by the company and used during the decades that Frisbie was in the region. Frisbie would use many of these ships in his stories. Of these schooners the *Tiare Taporo* was the most beloved and most famous throughout the region. It would be the ship that would appear the most in his articles and stories. The name was conceived by Donald, which suddenly came to him as he was indulging in some rum punches flavored by Tahitian limes. *Tiare Taporo* means, "lime blossom" in Tahitian. The ship was designed and built in 1913 by master shipwright, Charles Bailey Jr. of Auckland who was considered one of the foremost shipbuilders in New Zealand. The *Tiare Taporo* was fitted out with a trade room and a master and mate's cabins. Because of the large skylight that nearly ran the entire length of the ship, it was bright and airy. It was the last boat to be built specifically for trade in the islands. The boat ultimately wrecked at Aneityum in Vanuatu in 1968 ending her remarkable 55-year career as well as the era of trading schooners in the Pacific.

From left: Unknown man, Frisbie, Nordhoff, Harrison Smith, Viggo Rasmussen, a French doctor

The *Tiare Taporo* had two colorful, vivacious captains during Frisbie's time. Their names were Viggo Rasmussen and Andy Thompson. They were bigger than life and Frisbie loved them. He became good friends with them as he sailed, drank and caroused with them throughout the South Seas. Whenever they were in port, they would visit with Frisbie shooting-the-bull and drinking into the wee hours of the night. On occasion, as Frisbie got restless and needed a change, it was usually one of these two captains who transported him to another island. Frisbie even worked for them during voyages in the engine room, or utilized his navigational skills. The captains were real-life characters that defined a generation of schooner skippers in the Pacific. They were heroes to small boys and a best friend to the wayward beachcomber. Those who were fortunate enough to meet these two men had a tale or two to tell about them. Frisbie would use them in many of his stories. When they did appear in his writings, he never even changed their names.

Viggo Rasmussen was a short, stout man who was born in Denmark and went to sea at an early age arriving in Tahiti in 1896. He spent ten years in French Polynesia at various callings and came to know the islands, the people and their customs through his numerous trading schooner voyages as well as his pearling ventures in the Tuamotus. Like so many others who drifted to this corner of the South Seas, Rasmussen found the lifestyle very much to his liking. He romanced a girl from Mitiaro of the Cook Islands and married her. Eventually, he took his wife back to Mitiaro and set up a trading store on this tiny volcanic island that is only four miles across at its widest point. Rasmussen, however, belonged to the sea and its call proved to be too strong for him. He sailed away on the schooner *Vaite*, which would someday be replaced by the *Tiare Taporo*. He enjoyed trading throughout the Cook Islands because he knew that home was never far away.

The Pacific Islanders loved Rasmussen who was known as "Papa" to everyone. The trader, Tom Richards, once wrote that he never met a person like the genial Rasmussen who possessed so many fine characteristics. Rasmussen never had an enemy and never spoke any harsh words to his native crew or even raised his voice to issue a command. Many of the islands in the *Tiare Taporo*'s itinerary did not install a trader at a store, and so much of the business that Rasmussen conducted was transacted from the schooner. Copra was the main item that islanders possessed for trade. The supercargo would go to the island, weigh the copra and in exchange would hand out trade goods. Rasmussen was in charge of this trade. He possessed the dual qualifications of a sound businessman and a cool-headed skipper. He was also a pearl expert and ruled the great pearling lagoon of Penrhyn Island. It was said that because of his terrific standing with Penrhyn's natives no other firm would consider opening against him.

Rasmussen understood the islanders perfectly and had a wonderful knowledge of native dialects. In a letter to his mother dated February 23, 1923, Charles Nordhoff, described the sea captain to her:

> A schooner from the Cook Group just came in. The skipper is an extraordinary character—a Dane who has spent thirty years down here—is a profound authority on Oceanic philology, one of three or four living white men who speak fluently the strange old Paumotu language which some believe to be a link between India and the Inca civilization—a musician who spends hours discussing the fine points of Grieg-a cartographer who navigates with private charts made during his years of Pacific wandering—and a painter who works on entirely original theories and paints certain phases of sea and sky in a manner I have never seen excelled. He converses fluently in English, French, Danish, German, and any one of

half a dozen heathen dialects, and not the least endearing of his characteristics is a love of children known in all the remote places of Polynesia. When he heaves-to off an island, the entire juvenile population swarms off in canoes to swim to welcome Viggo.

One day I picked up the book, *Lost Island*, written by James Norman Hall. It was one of those books sitting in my collection that I had for years but couldn't remember if I had ever read it or not. The novel was published in 1944 and was a war story about an American engineer who was sent to a South Seas island to prepare the people and the island for the coming of a large American military force that will no doubt interrupt the daily life of the islanders. Early in the novel Hall introduced a character, the Resident Agent of an island by the name of Viggo, and obviously based on the Viggo Rasmussen that everyone knew and loved in the Pacific Islands. He described the character:

> His Christian name was Viggo and he was always called so, either that or "Papa Viggo." He was a Dane with a round ruddy face and hair so blond it was almost white.... There are certain men who, you know at first glance, are good all the way through. Viggo was one of these. I never heard him say an unkind word of anyone.

It is unknown how much the highly regarded captain knew about himself being used as a character in stories. But I get the feeling that the Dane would have never complained or opposed the use of his personality and would probably have a good, jolly laugh about it.

Andy Thompson was another colorful seafaring captain who became a legend by sailing the *Tiare Taporo* throughout the South Seas. He was known as Captain Andy and was born on January 21, 1885 in New York. Like Rasmussen, Thompson left home as a young boy to serve in the Atlantic trade aboard square-rigged ships. He also served as a quartermaster on ships that sailed the Great Lakes. When he was fifteen-years old, Thompson came to Rarotonga. He eventually married, raised a large family and made the island his home. When a couple of his sons grew to be teenagers, they became part of his crew. Although Thompson did not have much of a formal education, the copra schooners such as the *Tagua* and the *Tiare Taporo,* provided him with most of his education. He was enriched with more than thirty years of voracious reading during his long sea voyages, which gave him a wide range of interests.

Although Thompson met many men and women on his voyages, Frisbie held him in high esteem and the two of them became the greatest of friends. Thompson was the center of countless yarns and stories across the Pacific and no doubt Frisbie found them fascinating. It was reciprocal by the fact that many who were fortunate enough to meet Thompson had a tale or two to tell about the vibrant, unique captain. The Polynesian sailors loved Thompson because of his skilled seamanship and his record of never losing a man at sea. Hall once wrote about Thompson, "Whoever sails with Andy reaches his destination." Thompson was also an extremely generous man who helped many outer islanders (including Frisbie and his family) return home aboard his vessels even when they could not afford it.

I can recall when I first heard of the name of Andy Thompson. It was the second or third day of my arrival to Rarotonga and I was riding a bike (my usual form of transportation) through the capital town of Avarua. The unfamiliar sights and sounds of the town attracted me, forcing me to stop at whatever caught my fancy like the *Punanga Nui* market.

Not far from the market I remember riding past an unusual sight just east of the Avarua roundabout of what looked to be six or seven tall palm trees growing from one seed like a hydra of Greek Mythology. I immediately stopped to take a closer look and found that they were, indeed, growing from a single seed. I waited for a friendly looking passerby to ask if the tree had a name. This didn't take long as everyone in Rarotonga was friendly. But I did wait awhile to muster enough confidence to ask about the trees, as any shy guy would. Finally, I asked a woman who was walking by with two small children. She didn't know. The next person didn't know either. The third person didn't seem to understand me and looked at me like I was a crazed foreigner. Well, that was enough of that. My courage was lost. I hopped on my bike and peddled away to my next spot of interest. Later, I did learn that the trees were called Rarotonga's Seven Palms, and the seed was brought from an outer island in the early 1900's, and planted in the grounds of the Administration Building.

I was hoping that the tree had some captivating legend attached to it, something like it being the spot where seven great warriors fell in battle. No such luck. But there were three oral traditions associated with the tree. One of the legends linked the planting of the tree to a criminal trial in 1911 where a man was convicted of manslaughter and was sent to an outer island. Another man accompanied the exiled convict and brought the seven-sprout seed nut back to Rarotonga. The second story has the coconut tree being brought back in either Captain Thomas Harries or Captain Andy Thompson's schooner from another island. The third tradition has Andy Thompson recalling that Honorable William Estall brought the unique tree to Rarotonga from Manuae Atoll. Captain Andy remembered that the coconut was transferred from the wharf on a horse and buggy and was planted in the prominent site in front of the old Administration Building.

The mystery of the Seven Palms seemed to have been solved in 2005 when a written article was found and was about a person (Nia Rua) who was present at the planting of the tree. According to Rua the planting took place in 1907. She states that Resident Commissioner was so impressed with the tree that he had it planted in front of the Administration offices in the presence of all the students of Tereora College, including herself. Does the written record trump the oral traditions? Perhaps. But, it's still quite possible that the oral traditions played some kind of part of the coconut palm's history.

Frisbie was below deck when Rasmussen led him to the cabin-top and pointed out a narrow black line breaking briefly on the horizon and stated, "There's your Pukapuka." In Johnny's book, *The Frisbies of the South Seas*, she wrote that her father was on the schooner, *Tagua*. However, in the *Book of Puka-Puka* Frisbie wrote that he was sailing on the Tiare. Most likely it was the *Tagua* as that was the ship that Rasmussen was sailing at the time. The next morning the schooner was in the lee of the atoll, and when Frisbie came on deck, he noticed that a fresh trade wind ruffled the surface of the lagoon. He was at an end of the journey and the breeze seemed to want to carry him to this lonely place. The island was eerily quiet, as the islanders did not make much of a fuss over the arrival of the boat. Rasmussen noticed that Frisbie was lost in thought while gazing at the lethargic island and said, "The island is as dead asleep as it was before the three-fingered god Maui fished it out of the sea. Everything is asleep here. The people see no reason at all for getting up in the morning, and most of them don't. They sleep all day, but at night they wake-up, and you'll see them fishing by torchlight, eating, dancing and lovemaking on shore." Frisbie completely understood and nodded in total accordance with the islanders' circadian rhythm.

Pukapuka is located 652 nautical miles south of the equator and about 715 miles from Rarotonga. It consists of a group of three small islets connected by barrier reefs that enclosed a triangular lagoon about five miles long and one to two miles wide. The natives easily navigate the lagoon by paddle or sail, but they can also walk along the reefs. Wale is the islet at the north, and is shaped like a "Y." This is the main island where the entire population lives. At the southeast is a somewhat larger but less luxuriant U-shaped island known as Motu Ko. The smallest, elliptical islet to the southwest is Motu Kotawa. Pukapuka has an English name of Danger Island that was given by Commodore John Byron who sighted the island in 1765 and named it Islands of Danger because of the high surf that prevented landing. Today Pukapuka remains difficult to visit. There are no accommodations on the island and visitors will have to arrange a homestay with a local family through the island council. Air Rarotonga offers flights to the island but these flights are often infrequent and far between.

Another way to get there is by an inter-island cargo ship from Rarotonga; this may be quite an extensive and expensive journey, as the ship will visit other islands before reaching the atoll.

Since Frisbie spent nearly twenty-years on Pukapuka, and practically put the lonely islets on the map, it is worth spending a little more time describing the unique atoll. There are three settlements on the main island that are called Ngake (Windward), Roto (Central), and Yato (Leeward). The highest point on the islet is less than sixteen feet above sea level. The main vegetation that grows in abundance includes coconut palms, pandanus, puraka, which is a variety of taro that is tolerant to the environment, and breadfruit trees. Windward Village owns the large islet of Ko that produces more copra than the other two islets together. Leeward Village owns Frigate Bird Islet that is valuable because of the thousands of sea birds that nest there. The islet also has fine tract of guano where limes, breadfruit and mummy apples grow in abundance. Frisbie noted that despite their system of village land ownership, the Pukapukans all share alike and it is one of the few examples on earth of a "successful communistic government." There is no private ownership of land other than tracts upon which the houses are built. The land truly belongs to the villages and gives the islanders unlimited lease to live thereafter.

When Frisbie first glanced at Pukapuka islet on a bright sunlit morning, he instantly visualized himself in a cool roofed hut, his brow fanned by the trade winds and a charming Pukapukan would be ready to fill his pipe and call him to his meals. In his article titled, "Business as Usual," written in 1928, he proudly adds, "Contentment's motherly hand already seemed to rest on me soothingly. Here no officious relatives or friends would cry: Young man, you are wasting your life! Here you are nearing thirty, with nothing accomplished, with no plans for the future with no bank account! You must reform! It is your duty to keep the wheels of industry moving! Be efficient! Abstain from alcohol and tobacco! Join the church! Study Pelmanism!" Frisbie reveled in the opportunity of experiencing an unorthodox lifestyle. Pukapuka was perfect for him. He later stated that of all the islands in the South Seas, Pukapuka was his favorite and that he preferred living on an atoll to living on a high island. He felt that he really understood an atoll and that it held a palpable impression for him.

Frisbie was not the first white man who tried to settle on Pukapuka. A few months after his arrival, a native by the name of Kare, took him to the cemetery and pointed out three graves with white coral gravel banked over them. Coral slabs without any inscriptions enclosed the graves. The first grave was a Frenchman employed by a Samoan firm who killed himself in a fit of morbid nostalgia within three months of his arrival to the island. Next to him was the resting place of a missionary who also only lasted three months. Islanders believed that he went mad before he died. In the corner of the cemetery was a third grave of the white men. This man lasted six months on the atoll and legend has it that on his deathbed he swallowed a large diamond and half dozen pearls to make certain that they would be buried with him. When looking over the gravesites, Kare said to Frisbie, "Ah Ropati, they die very quickly indeed, just like that. You must be careful, Ropati, very, very careful. I advise you to learn the taboos and obey

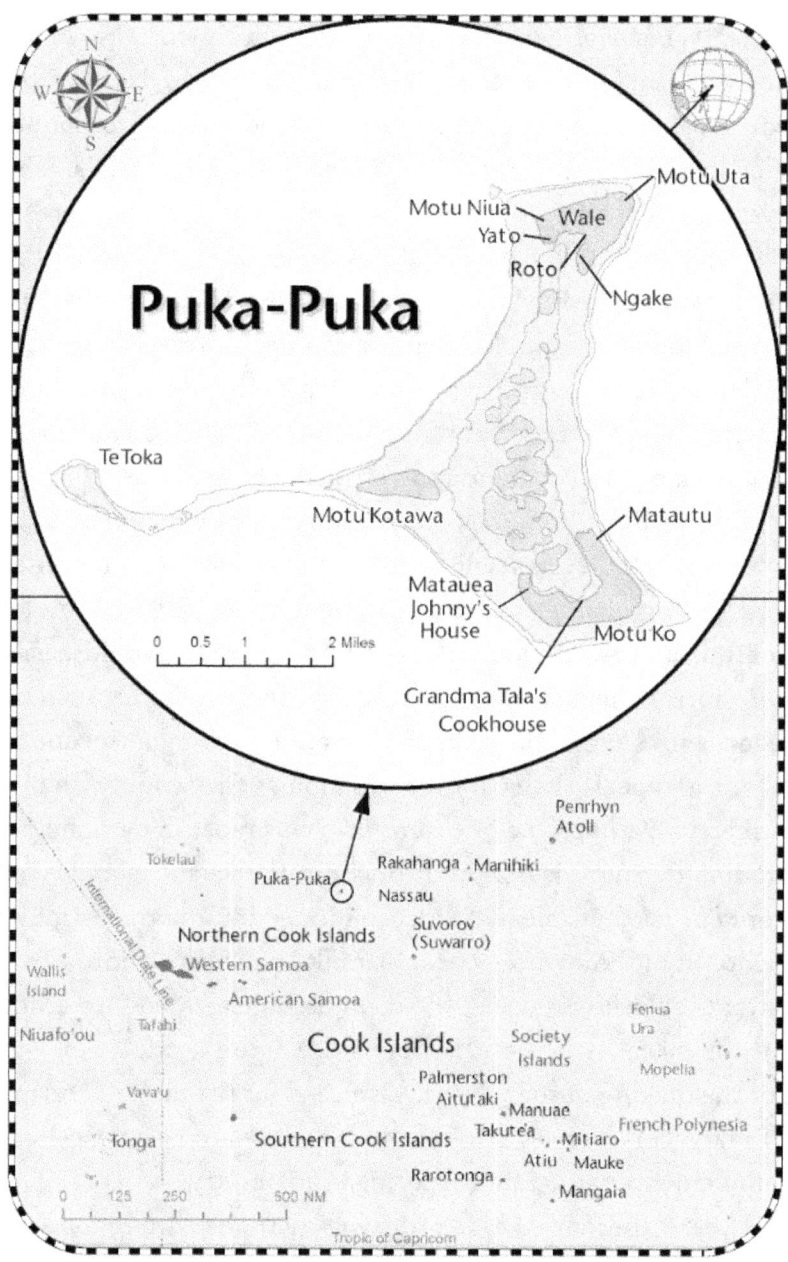

THEM. Whenever you are sick send quickly for the witch doctor. Also, I advise you, as a friend, never to go fishing after you have beaten your wife, and to avoid stealing coconuts during the full of the moon." Frisbie noted that Kare's fishy eyes stared at an empty space beyond the Frenchman's grave. Then he unconsciously turned toward Frisbie and back at the empty space. Frisbie knew what was going on in his mind but it was time to leave and open the trading store. As they were walking out of the graveyard, Kare gave Frisbie one last bit of advice, "Also, Ropati, you must read the Bible, go to church, and cook no food on Sunday. Every little thing helps."

The traders for A.B. Donald Company were managers that operated retail stores selling mainly very basic commodities and fishing gear. Because the trading boats visited some of these island so infrequently, the trading stores would easily run out of their stock, especially on popular items such as flour and sugar. The islanders would exchange coconuts, pearls and pearl shells. If they had money, they could also buy products. Perhaps the one item that was most in demand for trading during this period throughout the Pacific Islands was copra or coconut meat. As a coconut aged in the tree, a milky white liquid known as coconut milk transformed into flesh. After the flesh was dried, the copra is transformed into crude oil and oil cakes. The most popular use of the extracted oil was for the making of soap. It was also used for the manufacturing of margarine and vegetable fats, and proved to be an excellent supplementary food for cattle, pigs and poultry.

There are many kinds of drying methods throughout the world where copra was made. In the Pacific Islands the preferred method of drying was simply by the sun which was the slowest, yet easiest method of copra manufacture. Typically, coconuts were never picked, but allowed to fall naturally to the ground and collected for processing. On many Pacific Islands the fallen coconuts were split in halves and placed on the bare ground. Then the kernels were arranged to face upwards to catch the direct rays of the sun. If persistent rain showers occurred, the coconuts could be turned over facing the ground and piled on top of each other.

On Pukapuka the harvesting of copra would be an annual event where every villager would get involved and help with the drying process. In her book, *The Frisbies of the South Seas,* Johnny remembered this annual event as a "copra festival" that took place from November through March. The villagers would sail their canoes across the lagoon to Motu Kotawa or Motu Ko where they would rebuild the old racks and construct new ones for drying coconuts. Families then picked a small section of the coconut trees and the competition began. Villagers were paid only for the amount of nuts they actually collected and turned into copra. Anybody could fight over untouched coconuts, which often led to amusing arguments and long discussions over a single nut.

The coconuts were then husked, cut in halves and the spongy centers were scooped out and placed in a basket for eating. The shells were taken to the beach where they were soaked in the sea so that the meat would be tougher and less liable to rot during the drying process. After a couple of days of soaking in the sea, the shells were taken out and laid on the wooden racks with the meat facing the sun. If it rained, everyone would help turn the shells over to prevent the meat from getting wet.

The coconuts would take several weeks to dry, and once they did, the meat was spooned out, cut into small pieces and placed in copra sacks. Johnny recalls everyone having a good time while they waited for the meat to cure, as villagers sung, danced and played American games such as baseball and poker that her father had taught them.

Producing copra was practically the only thing that natives did to make a living. It was used to buy the few goods from the "outside world" that they desired such as canned corned beef or a twist of tobacco. Interestingly, during the cruise of the *Janet Nichol* in May of 1890, Robert Louis Stevenson's wife, Fanny, was taking notes for her husband and made this observation when the boat approached Pukapuka:

> As we drew near, the three islands of the group began to detach themselves. Danger Island, or Pukapuka, is the only one inhabited. It is governed by a king who allows none of his subjects to gather coconuts without his royal permission, and as he seldom lets anyone have more than is sufficient for his food, very little copra is made. Here the nuts, contrary to the usual custom, are dried in the shell to prevent cockroaches from devouring the meat, and consequently the copra is very fine and white; but the quantity made is so small that it does not pay to keep a trader on the island.

Attitudes toward the trading station definitely changed on Pukapuka atoll by the time Frisbie arrived. The trading stores throughout Polynesia varied. Some of the stores were nothing more than a shed while others were larger. Frisbie described his trading post on Pukapuka as a two-story building with thick walls made from blocks of chipped coral. There were two large rooms on the ground floor and two living quarters on the second floor. The second-floor rooms opened to verandahs that faced the front of the house as well as the back. The front verandah overlooked the road and the central village, while the back balcony faced the lagoon and was only a few feet from the water's edge. Frisbie truly enjoyed his verandahs and utilized them every day.

When Frisbie sat on the back balcony, he was cooled by the trade-winds and easily lost himself in a sleepy fantasy. His daydream would eventually be broken by either a voice at the front of the building, or the crowing of a rooster, or the monotonous drumming on coconut shells by the village children. At night he preferred sitting on his front verandah where he could watch village life passing below him. He quickly discovered that on this island the islanders awoke at sunset and stumbled sleepily into the lagoon for a bath. After they had refreshed themselves, they started the activities of the day. The village came to life at night. Frisbie noted that as sunset turned to night, fisherman put out in canoes with torches and a net for flying-fish, while others held spears for lobsters and parrot-fish of the reef. Fires flared among the houses and groups of chattering islanders strolled up and down the village street.

In *The Book of Puka-Puka* Frisbie eloquently wrote about what happened as the night wore on:

At about ten o'clock the fishing canoes returned. Then, like magic, the islet was transformed. Scores of coconut-shell fires blazed with their characteristic glaring white flame, throwing grotesque shadows on the brown thatched huts, dancing in fairylike shimmerings among the domes of coconut fronds, casting ghostly reaches of light through the adjacent graveyards, and silhouetting the forms of pareu-clad natives at work cleaning their fish or laying them on the live coals to broil.

He added that everything on the island was dreamlike and that the island itself was a dream come true for such a romanticist as him. Within a short time, he truly felt that his faith in a lonely land beyond the farthest horizon was, indeed, vindicated.

I can recall during my time in Rarotonga that there wasn't much to do at night on the island. Like most of the towns in the region, the sidewalks rolled up at five o'clock. After work, many of my volunteer colleagues would patronize a bar, or find a restaurant where they feasted on crab soaked in coconut milk. But, for me, I enjoyed finding a secluded spot to daydream. So I walked to the beach and planted myself in the sand. The sound of the waves crashing against the reef was in the distance and the repetitive rumble was quite soothing. The trade-winds slapped me in the face and it not only kept me comfortable on a balmy night, it also kept the mosquitoes from harassing me.

What I remember the most though was the night sky and how the millions of stars literally entertained me. It was truly a night spectacular and I felt like the only one in the audience. It was my own personal show. The stars were an awesome sight and every fifteen minutes or so one would plunge to the sea like a dying skyrocket. I made a wish. I had a lot of wishes during my stay on the island. I searched for the Southern Cross, the simple star constellation that has come to symbolize the South Seas. Like Frisbie on his verandah, I easily submerged myself in deep thought asking myself what I wanted to do with my life and what dreams do I want to accomplish. From this time onward, I made a conscious effort to take in the night sky no matter which Pacific Island I happened to be visiting.

The "trader life" was the good life on Pukapuka. It was hard to imagine a better way to spend the day, and Frisbie took full advantage of it. And why not? The Pukapukans lifestyle was one of lying under a coconut tree and sleeping. Indubitably they were untroubled by the desire for worldly goods and the need to work for them. Time seemed to stand still on this little atoll. Who cared what year it was? Frisbie remained ambitious but was also in complete sympathy with the Pukapukan way of life. Although he was mostly penniless, his assured but paltry army income helped him in times of desperation. He realized that if he made enough to eat, be clothed, slept under a roof and had a girlfriend, life was good.

Frisbie was the first white trader to open a store in fourteen years. He was easygoing and his simple methods of handling sales made him a popular figure on the island. Frisbie remembered his first day working at the store and his encounter with the first customer. It was a child who peeped around the edge of the door holding a coconut out at arm's length. He recalled, "... just as our first customer was about to make a purchase, his courage failed him and he rushed whooping away." After this small incident, he closed the store. But as day turned to night, the villagers began to awake, and before Frisbie knew it, there was a small crowd waiting to come into the store.

Frisbie enjoyed watching the islanders buy things on this opening day. Some of them did not know how to use money, but he resolved almost immediately to never cheat the island folk. A man by the name of Ezekiel laid a pound note on the counter and bought talcum powder, thus becoming Frisbie's very first customer. Frisbie later wrote, "I soon learned all the peculiarities of the Puka-Puka trade. Success depended upon stocking the store with articles of no earthly use to the islanders." The store ran out of talcum powder on the first day and Shampoo d'Or on the second day. Perfume was also very popular and large quantities were used internally as medicine. Frisbie once witnessed a villager pour a whole bottle of it over himself after his salt-water bath. "Then he was off to the sea side of the islet, where, no doubt, he was highly successful in his lovemaking."

Despite living a carefree lifestyle, Frisbie made sure to never turn "native." In his book, *The Island of Desire*, he explained the importance of keeping his status as a white man:

> When a white man goes native the people brand him as no better than themselves. He will find that soon the natives will look down on him. Why shouldn't they? He cannot compete with them in their own culture. If he tries to do these things he makes himself ridiculous, and is plainly inferior to the natives. But he can, by living as a white man, prove his foreign culture to be, in many ways, superior to the native culture. I mean

only that in his general attitude toward life he should remain true to his race.

Frisbie believed that natives should be proud of their white man and that they should admire and brag about him.

The Pukapukan language came naturally to Frisbie. All Polynesian languages are closely related and since he had a fairly good knowledge of Tahitian and Rarotongan, he was able to learn Pukapukan quite quickly. He stated that within three months he was able to speak the language with considerable fluency. The only difficulty he had was when he tried to follow islander's conversations that slurred words or expressed themselves in obscure Pukapukan metaphors. Today English is widely spoken throughout the Cook Islands as children are taught from an early age. Back in 2002 the main mission of the Global Volunteers that I was involved with on Rarotonga was to teach the school children how to read in English. It was of high importance for the volunteer mission, although I admit that I was quite oblivious about the entire project at first because I was busy working in libraries.

Little did I know that within a week I would have to fill-in and help teach the kids to read in addition to my library jobs, as about half of our team became ill. I can recall biking to Takitumu School trying my best to beat the rain and the numerous giant dogs that, for some odd reason, loved to chase me as if I had bacon tied to my back tire. Unfortunately, during this time a mosquito-borne tropical disease known as Dengue Fever was running through the island, and it seemed it was hitting my fellow volunteers indiscriminately. The symptoms were very similar to the flu, such as achy joints, fever, vomiting, and a skin rash. A little paranoia swept through our camp. It was quite exciting as we wondered who would be the next poor soul to contract the disease. Those of us who were still standing bonded together with nervous bravado.

To this day I doubt that my colleagues actually had Dengue, and believe that it was just a stomach flu of some kind that was spreading around from person to person. Whatever it was I never caught it. If anything, it made a good story, one that I still enjoy telling to this day. I felt like the last man standing. More importantly, teaching the kids wasn't that bad. They turned out to be a lot of fun. I played soccer, net ball and other games with them and they would visit me working in the school's library. I admit that I actually could not wait to get to school each morning despite being soaked or harassed by giant, man-eating dogs. It was all part of the adventure.

Frisbie claimed that after he learned the language there was very little for him to do in his leisure hours. And so he kept busy writing and reading. He enjoyed reading all day long, day after day. His mother and brother would send him books, and after a couple of years, Frisbie's library grew, covering a space on the wall six feet high and eight feet long. He studied each author's style thoroughly, and because he was more interested in style rather than narrative, he would read a book over and over. He devoured the classics such as, the *D'artagnan Romances, The Three Musketeers, Twenty Years After, Louise de la Valliere, Decameron,* and the *Man in the Iron Mask.* Frisbie also kept stacks of magazines that were sent to him from the United States and Tahiti. Whatever reading material he could get his hands on he would read. As an oral society, the islanders were perplexed with his incessant attention to the written word. He would also read poetry aloud to the natives, many of who would peep from the doors and windows like curious cats.

Besides engaging in island activities like fishing trips, bird catching, and even moonlight diversions on the beach, he never lost focus on his dream of writing the great novel. During these early years on the Pukapuka he wrote an increasing abundance of material. In 1927 *Sunset* magazine published an article titled, "Why I Enjoy Armchair Yachting." The publication earned him $125, but more importantly, it gave him newfound inspiration and confidence. Other publications soon followed. The *Atlantic Monthly* published "At Home in Puka-Puka" and "Kanaka Voyage." The *St. Nicholas,* magazine paid him for the title, "The Seas Afire," which was about torch fishing for flying fish on Pukapuka. Then one of the most satisfying and happiest moments in his life took place in 1929 when the Century Company published almost thirty sketches of his under the title, *The Book of Puka-Puka.*

Today *The Book of Puka-Puka* is widely considered a South Seas classic. If there is one book that Frisbie will be remembered for, it is this one. While reviewing the book Nordhoff wrote, "As I laid down the book last night and blew out my reading-lamp, I said to myself, *If this isn't true, it ought to be, and from what I know of Frisbie, and have heard of Puka Puka, it probably is.* He added that the book presented a wonderful portrait of Frisbie himself. The selection of material came from a vast diary of his day-to-day experiences and observations. "There was no dullness, no inane scientific babble by a layman, and there was little left out in the doings and sayings of the Pukapukans." Indeed, the book was an eloquent description of the islanders. Nordhoff continued his review by stating, "The author writes as a native and not as a traveler, and perhaps this is the foundation of the book's charm. The combination of qualities that make such writing possible is rare: imagination, close observation, a feeling for beauty, and a thoroughly page point-of-view are some of them."

Frisbie's first book was full of sketches, closely-knit and drawing with seeming random lines and bits of light and shadow. The vignettes captured a life that was quite remote from that of the world at large as to be almost unimaginable. He dedicated the book to his friend and mentor, James Norman Hall. Each chapter was preceded by a short chant in the native language and translated into English. According to Natasa Potocnik's 2011 paper, "Robert Dean Frisbie: Writer of the South Seas: His Contribution to Pacific Literature," she described *The Book of Puka-Puka* stating that Frisbie had no qualms about criticizing European and American commercialism and aggressiveness. Potocnik added that he displayed popular themes such as: the praise of isolation, the chastisement of missionaries, the commendation of Polynesian economic collectivism and sexual freedom. The book showed how well he assimilated with the culture of Pukapuka in front of a colorful and tropical environment. The tone and spirit of the book was very much compared to that of the South Seas life of artist Paul Gauguin.

The *Book of Puka-Puka* was my first introduction to Frisbie. At first, I thought the book was fiction until I learned more about the author and his life. It was one of those books that I couldn't put down. I was enthralled and intrigued with the way he came to the island, learned the language and interacted with the natives. His adventures on the tiny island were utterly mind-blowing. I thought, how many people in this world would give up everything and go to the South Pacific in the 1920s? How many would or can do it today? Naturally books and stories are supposed to make readers ask questions—many questions in some cases. They are supposed to transcend a reader to another time and world. The islanders of *The Book of Puka-Puka* were more than just characters; they were real, and Frisbie enjoyed writing about them. Eventually, I understood the fascination that Frisbie had with his fellow island dwellers. Pacific Islanders are some of the most colorful people on earth. Frisbie was amused and annoyed by them. But, overall, he adored his island neighbors and often created nicknames for them in his stories such as Mama, Sea Foam, Bones, Little Sea, Wail-of-Woe, Desire, King-of-the-Sky, and his best friend, William-the-Heathen.

CHAPTER FOUR
DESIRE AND THE COWBOYS

Although *The Book of Puka-Puka* briefly gave Frisbie confidence to continue writing, he did not believe that he had found success in the profession. Living on the island for many years had made him weary and not having many people to converse with, made him a bit self-centered. He began to look bitterly at the world. He thought about leaving the island for either Tahiti or Rarotonga in hopes of engaging in conversations with men that he was more accustomed to in these ports. To solve some of these problems, Frisbie thought it would be a good idea to take a wife and settle down.

Frisbie began to take more of an interest in his friendly rendezvous with a petite, beautiful and devoted Polynesian girl named, Ngatokorua-a-Mataa. He eventually fell in love with her. She was only fifteen at the time. Johnny defended her mother's young age when she wrote: a Pukapukan girl is a mature woman long before she passes her teens.

Frisbie's courtship with Ngatokorua was unlike anything

he could have imagined or he could have ever experienced while living in the United States. In his stories he often referred to Ngatokorua as Desire. Frisbie recounts one of his first nights with her as he watched her dance in his book *The Island of Desire*. He wrote, "Her grass skirt had been made by Tangi from the whitest of bleached fiscus bark; it was so bushy that it accentuated the width of her hips and her movement in the dance." He continued in such a way that would make any western young man quickly head to the South Seas at the sniff of any opportunity, much like the sailors did in the 18th and 19th centuries: "Her breasts were bare, to me they were soft, round, inviting. With her mind on the movements of the dance, a little scowl puckering her brow and the bridge of her nose, she danced as though she were a priestess officiating in her temple, as perhaps she was." Johnny would later question this passage doubting that her mother danced barebreasted and that her father was most likely exaggerating to entice his readers. Nevertheless, the couple would take long strolls with their arms around each other's waists until they found a little path that led into the magnolia bush. These paths were known as the "love nests" of the young unmarried.

Frisbie was curious and fascinated with the sexual prowess of the young on Pukapuka. After all, he was still in his twenties when he first arrived on the atoll and beautiful, exotic Polynesian women were hard to ignore. Frisbie talked about the morality of the Pukapukans and stated that adultery was practically unknown throughout the island noting that before young people married, they were given unlimited freedom to find temporary mates. "I believe that they become sated with sex when young, leaving them with no desire for amorous adventures in middle life," he said. Frisbie was convinced that this sexual freedom of the young people between the ages of fourteen and eighteen was the direct cause of their fidelity after they had selected a permanent mate. He wrote, "They have unlimited opportunity to become intimately acquainted with each other, thus lessening the possibility of post-connubial disillusionment." He felt that this philosophy worked well on a small atoll where malignant diseases were not common.

There were times when Frisbie felt like an anthropologist examining the sexual attitudes and relationships of the people on a remote Pacific Island's atoll. He was especially captivated by the "love fests" of the young unmarried and gracefully wrote in *The Book of Puka-Puka*:

> At night there are shadows in the coconut-groves of Puka-Puka—lacelike shadows of fronds, shadows of stiff-limbed pandanus-trees, of ground bush, and of the fleecy trade-wind clouds skimming low overhead. And there are the shadows of the young unmarried, wide awake now and slipping from tree to tree on their way to the love fests on the sea side of the islet.

Frisbie recalls attending a love fest and came to the spot where the young unmarried were gathered. A wailing heathen strain was heard from the bush as a boy drummed a weird rhythm on a coconut-shell while a couple danced before him. "I could hear laughing cries from out on the reef and see shadowy figures here and there." Frisbie noticed that there were no spying chaperons, spoil-sports or moralizing parents to hinder the wild youth in their adventures or to prevent them from understanding each other as God must have meant them to. "If there is any place on earth where men and women live naturally, surely it is on Puka-puka."

Ngatokorua was the fourth child of a native missionary who sailed to Pukapuka from Rarotonga on the *John Williams* to help build one of the first mission churches on the island. This was a remarkable feat considering that it was done at the turn of the 20th century and the only way to chart the course was to simply navigate using the sun and the stars. This was the story for all Pacific Islanders who were settling in the islands during the region's migration period and Ngatokorua's father's accomplishment probably did not seem like a big deal to the islanders at the time. Nevertheless, the missionary's achievement was eventually Frisbie's gain. He was absolutely smitten by Ngatokorua. Frisbie recalls that during their first late night tryst Ngatokorua said to him, "You are one of the wild youths now. Why don't you take a new name?"

"You think of one for me," Frisbie responded.

Without hesitation Ngatokorua explained, "I have done it already. You told me you would come for me when the moon was full, and now you are with me alone for the first time with the moonlight shining on us, so I am going to call you Mr. Moonlight."

"That's a nice name. What is your nickname in the House of Young Women?"

"I am Miss Memory."

"What ceremony on Yato Beach. Frisbie's disdain for organized religions and clergyman caused him to not invite the bride's father and many others to the ceremony. The only two witnesses that were present were one of Ngatokorua's sisters and William-the-Heathen who also presided over the wedding. William-the-Heathen was Frisbie's best friend on the island. As an ex-whaler, William learned a little English aboard various ship. The two spent hours together sharing bush beer and philosophically discussing a variety of life and island life topics.

Bush beer was a type of elixir made from imported yeast, malt, hops and sugar. The lethal concoction was made from fermented bananas (and these days oranges, or just an orange-flavored juice) in a hollowed-out coconut tree stump called a *tumunu*. The drink itself had a very strong alcohol level, and the longer it was kept, the stronger it got. Today tourists who visit the Cook Islands like to seek out and sample bush beer. Some of the islands such as Atiu, attract visitors to *tumunu* huts where a barman will give a short prayer, introduces the drinkers to each other, and then allows everyone to share stories about where they came from. Music from bands and individual musicians with ukuleles will eventually join in the festivities. The *tumunu* hut has become a social tourist destination.

William was kind of a safety net for Frisbie. Whenever Frisbie got fed up with native life, he would call on William, who told him ribald tales of his youth and was a living "Who's Who" in regards to all the characters living on Pukapuka. Frisbie never tired of his company. William was the only one on the island who had the courage to disregard the missionaries and their preaching. Although William was in his eighties, Frisbie believed that the reprobate was ageless. Often during times of long discussion, the old heathen would suddenly leap to his feet and impressively shimmy up a coconut tree for drinking nuts agilely as a monkey, or he would begin to move with youthful energy through one of the dances of pagan times.

Frisbie was always amazed with William and his impeccable timing. He recalled in one of his articles that one night he returned to his wattle-and-thatch house on the lagoon beach and began singing. He often sung to himself whenever he felt he was alone. Midway through his song he heard someone exclaim, "Nonsense!" from the heavy foliage of his ceiling. Frisbie looked up and saw William lying among the palm fronds.

"Why, William, I thought you had gone home!" Frisbie remarked.

"I sleep here nowadays, and I don't like to be bothered by lubbers who sing out of tune," William said.

"You sleep in the roof?"

"No mosquitos here. The rest of the people will start sleeping on the outer beach when their mosquito nets rot away."

Frisbie was never perturbed or shocked at the behavior of his odd opinionated companion. He anticipated William's mood and antagonized him at every opportunity. Frisbie's meetings with William must have been a great source of amusement especially on those endless and lethargic days.

At Frisbie's wedding William functioned as witness and minister who officiated the ceremony. He tried to act as professional as possible asking the important questions to both bride and groom on how they will take care of each other. Frisbie worried a little bit about not having the island's priest to conduct the matrimony mostly because he did not want to hear any complaints from the dissatisfied clergyman. He was also in a hurry for William to finish the proceeding because he was anxious to sail across the lagoon with his new bride. He ordered, "Now would you give us a paper to sign and get this over with?" He then handed William a braid of tobacco. "Here. Give this twist of tobacco to Parson Kare Moana. And here's some for your pipe." Then the two men shook hands. "Goodbye William. We are sailing away!" The couple sailed for Motu Ko which was about four miles across the lagoon.

In the book, *The Island of Desire*, Frisbie wrote that Yato Point would make an ideal place to a build a permanent home for himself. He believed it would be perfect because it was well away from Leeward Village and there was usually a fresh trade wind that blew across the lagoon. The islet was clean, free from mosquitoes and had a fine bathing beach. He asked himself, "Why suffer in Central Village?" His presence at the trading station was required for only twenty days or so a year, and he had a chest full of silver shillings and pound notes. "Why not spend some of them for the health of my soul?" He also thought how nice it would be to lead his bride to a beautiful home instead of to the musty trading station.

By June 1929 Frisbie was feeling restless and was itching to travel again. Ngatokorua had never been outside of Pukapuka and Frisbie was determined to show her other parts of the Pacific. He decided to take his wife to Rarotonga and Tahiti and the couple took advantage at seeking passage on the *Tiare Taporo* that happened to be at the island. It was perfect timing and Frisbie could not wait to show his wife part of the "outside world." Viggo Rasmussen was captaining the schooner at the time and was pleased to have his old friend aboard. It also appeared that the trader Tom Richards was on board serving as the supercargo and noticed the "gangly, well-known American writer." He wrote about the encounter in his book, *White Man, Brown Woman*. Although Richards never mentioned Frisbie by his name in the book, Frisbie was the only white man on Pukapuka at the time.

Tiare Taporo

The trader turned supercargo recalled that the *Tiare Taporo* was the first vessel that had called at Pukapuka for two years. He observed that Frisbie was glad of the opportunity to talk in his own language because he was the only American resident on the island. He also noted that Frisbie had married a Pukapukan woman and settled down to the isolation of the last place on earth. Richards believed that after a brief conversation with the American, that Frisbie disliked his environment and always talked lovingly of America, but never hinted that he might go back some day. Something kept him in the islands and even Rasmussen could not drag that reason from him.

Richards was unimpressed with Ngatokorua as well as Pukapukan woman in general. He felt that they were the lowest type of natives in the Eastern Pacific. They wore scarcely any clothes and had appalling habits. He thought, "They are a curious race, and speak little, making themselves understood by movements of the lips." He was being unnecessarily harsh as other writers and photographs have shown that the appearance of a Pukapukan woman was quite exquisite. Richards studied the couple on their way to Rarotonga. He was intrigued and shocked at Ngatokorua's unusual display of affection towards Frisbie. He described the event, "She took the lobe of his ear between her teeth, and bit it until the blood ran freely. Frisbie would yell out sharply and she would laugh until she cried at his discomfort. She indulged in this habit particularly at mealtimes."

After they arrived in Rarotonga, Richards was amused when Frisbie bought his wife her first pair of boots and shoes. She liked them so much that she refused to take them off at bedtime and they had to be removed by force. Johnny would later comment on this behavior stating that she believed that no Pukapukan woman would bite her husband's ear in public and that her mother was too sophisticated to sleep with boots on. I could also attest to Johnny's statement because every Pacific Island woman that I ever met on my visits was nothing short of composure and grace. We both agreed that Richards was, perhaps, exaggerating for the sake of the readers of his book and wanted to let readers know that he knew the American author very well.

Although Frisbie feared that his wife would not grow

accustomed to a new environment and become homesick, their time in Rarotonga was one of the happiest moments of their married lives. They found a secluded house in the island's capital town, Avarua, that was surrounded by coconut trees and which reminded them of Pukapuka. They enjoyed getting out and exploring the craggy, mountainous interior. Their long hikes must have fascinated Ngatokorua who had never seen land higher than the few feet elevation on Pukapuka. Their happiness grew even more when on June 23, 1930 Ngatokorua gave birth to a baby boy that they named Charles Mata'a (Charles from Frisbie's brother and Mata'a from Ngatokorua's father). However, Frisbie did not stay long to enjoy his first born as he had planned a trip to San Francisco to visit his brother even before the birth of his son.

Johnny wrote that while her father was in San Francisco he did embark on a little adventure. He took passage aboard a three-masted schooner, *Marchal Foch* that was bound for Mexico. As this was during the time of Prohibition, the boat was to load its hull with containers of rum and other alcoholic beverages and sneak them back to San Francisco. These smuggling ships would anchor three to twelve miles beyond the maritime limit, just outside major ports all along the Atlantic and Pacific seaboard. The line of ships was known as "Rum Row." These small, quick boats could easily outrun Coast Guard ships, and if need be, could dock in any small river or eddy and transfer their cargo to a waiting truck. Frisbie would eventually write about his "Rum Running" adventures in an article titled, "Rum Row: Western," which was published by the *Atlantic Monthly* in 1932.

About this time Frisbie was also aboard a five-masted schooner that he called, "Rum-Runner Extraordinary." On

August 17, 1931 he wrote a letter to his friend James Hall a few days sail from the coast of Vancouver. He opened the letter by joking with the *Bounty*, writer that he hoped that Hall was keeping sober and having no more children to burden his old days and bringing premature grey hairs to his head. (Hall had two children, a son and a daughter.) Frisbie told Hall that he was not sure how long he would be away but it seemed that he did not mind being away from his wife and newborn son. The adventurer in him was never more evident:

> ....Captain Stone suggests that I sail with him for as long as I care to, perhaps going to Halifax, St. Pierre and the West Indies; perhaps to Tahiti. But it's chilly up here even now, and I may have to make a quick jump to the islands to warm up. I can do this boarding one of the subchaser rum boats at dark of night, off a lonely cove on the California coast; then to Rum Row where I can wait for a Papeete schooner. This will be much nicer than boarding a damned steamboat and sailing to Tahiti like a normal fool.

The tone of his letter to Hall suggested that he was really enjoying his, what he termed "lecherous adventures" on the Rum Runner. It was the money, however, that played a major impetus of him getting a job on such a ship as he told Hall that he only had forty to fifty dollars to his name. He believed that he would collect a few grand for this adventure. If he did go broke, he believed there was a job waiting for him in one of the "rum in" boats at six hundred a month plus eighty cents a case. "After a few days of this I can lam to the islands filthy rich." It was never reported how much money he actually made during these "Rum Running" excursions, but it does not appear that he got rich from it. Money problems would plague him for the rest of his life. Some people are destined to become rich and some are not. Fortunately, there are other ways to prosper in life. It should not always be about the money. The secret to a happy life is to always have something to look forward to and Frisbie constantly looked to the future even during the toughest of times.

As he made his way to Vancouver, Frisbie did report in a letter to Hall that he had time to work on a couple of stories. He described the two stories to Hall as "The islands one, and a story about rum running." He had hoped to write another before reaching Vancouver and even thought about taking his stories personally to his publisher in New York. Frisbie ended his letter by telling Hall the latest book that he read was *The Old Curiosity Shop* by Charles Dickens. "What a book!" No man living today can write like that—anything like that, Hall *tane*." Tane meant "man" in Maori. In Maori and other Polynesian mythology *Tane* was the god of forests and light and by some accounts created man.

The trip to San Francisco convinced Frisbie that the Pacific Islands, particularly Pukapuka, was the best place for him to live. He felt that he had lost touch with civilization forever and that he had nothing in common with the people of his own race. He believed that people could not understand a person who chained himself to no itinerary. On the ship back to Rarotonga he wrote to his brother and stated, "Except for the memory of you and one or two others, the whole stay in San Francisco seems like a fantastic dream, a wild nightmare of fat hangdog little men puffing as they try to work hard enough to please their raw-boned damned women." This seemed bitter. Perhaps he was strained and upset for not making the amount of money he had hoped while working on the Rum Runner.

Frisbie continued to defend his way of life by writing that he had lived in Pukapuka so long that his acts were governed by feeling and not by reason. He said, "I do not feel that my life is futile, and I do not court regret by reasoning about it; and there is at least the element of surprise which is lacking in orderly existence. Why make a task rather than a pleasure of life?" His defensive and bitter attitude turned to utter bewilderment upon his return to Rarotonga when he learned that his son, Charles, was adopted by Ngatokorua's aunt, Piki-Piki, and she refused to give the baby back.

Adoption or multiple parenting in Polynesia was actually quite a common practice. This meant that there were a number of people who would be involved in the raising of the child. Siblings, cousins and aunts often adopted one another's children and even grandparents would adopt their own grandchildren. Adoption increased the flexibility within the family by accruing additional parents to a child rather than just simply replacing the child's biological parents. To the Polynesians there were a number of benefits for multiple parenting. One of these benefits was that the deaths of parents became less of a crisis. Another blessing showed that children were protected from parental incompetence especially during an intolerable marriage. On the flip side multiple parenting reduced stress on parents. The old maxim, "many hands make light work," also makes happy babies, and when babies are happy, parents are happy. Naturally Frisbie did not understand this custom especially when it was applied to his own child. He threatened Piki-Piki's life but was calmed by

Ngatokorua who told him how normal it was in the islands. Frisbie would not see Charles again until 1943 when he resettled on Rarotonga.

Shortly after his return to Rarotonga, Frisbie needed money and partnered with a former British Captain, J. A. Bunting, in a copra venture. Frisbie thought that copra might be more lucrative than writing. The two men left for Manuae Island, about 124 miles northeast, with eighteen Rarotongan laborers who were used to plant coconut trees and make copra. The island was another tropical paradise as it was swarming with edible sea birds and the lagoon and sea was teeming with fish. The two men spent most of their time in the water. Frisbie found himself thinking about writing stories about the island rather than thinking about how the island can increase copra production; the venture inevitably fizzled out. After a few weeks, he headed back to Rarotonga. The adventure on Manuae Island was not a total loss as it did provide him with the idea to write an article titled, "A Copra Island," which was published by the *Atlantic Monthly* in 1932.

Frisbie was eager to show his wife more of the Pacific Islands and the two sailed away with Captain Andy Thompson to Tahiti. The trip to Tahiti was a harrowing, yet invigorating, sail where they covered seven hundred miles in four days through a raging squall. During the grueling trip Ngatokorua became seasick and scared and predominantly remained in her cabin. One day she mustered enough courage and energy to look out the porthole of her cabin and noticed that her husband was reveling in this adventure. Frisbie turned and smiled at her and she immediately felt better. When she would look out the same porthole again within a couple of days, she gave a sigh of relief as she saw the green, craggy mountains of Tahiti.

Frisbie and his wife settled down to a pleasant and peaceful lifestyle in Tahiti. They lived with two brothers named Schumacher, in a two-story house that was perched on a ledge on the side of a mountain. Like on Rarotonga the couple explored the rich, damp valleys and lounged at the beaches and bays. Frisbie's health was good during the early period of their Tahiti stay. He even dedicated a lot of time to his writing. The *Atlantic Monthly* published his first fiction tale titled, "Th e Ghost of Alexander Perks, A.B." which was about a ghost who haunted a trading schooner. It was a classic ghost story that could easily find its way in any anthology of ghost stories today.

Frisbie also started another book, *My Tahiti*, and worked on two unpublished autobiographical novels titled, *Andre Moreau* and *Teanua*. Johnny noted that during this creative period of her father's he liked to seek fair criticism of his work. He wanted someone with experience to critique his work, and thus, turned to his old friend Hall. Hall felt that *My Tahiti* was not quite ready for publication and encouraged Frisbie to keep working on it. Hall's constructive criticism, although harsh, was quite helpful to Frisbie. When Hall critiqued *Teanua*, he found the use of split infinitives annoying, and raved to Frisbie, "...perhaps, you will be able to write in ten years' time!" When he came upon a scene deeper within the same manuscript that described a distant relative of Teanua on Penrhyn pacing the deck during a hurricane and shaking his fists heavenward and cursing God, Hall continued his criticism and stated, "This is he-man stuff, so maybe you will make it in nine and a half years."

MR. MOONLIGHT OF THE SOUTH SEAS

Ngatokorua and Daughter Johnny

On June 19, 1932 the first of three Frisbie daughters was born in a Papeete hospital. Ngatokorua wanted to name the baby, Ngatokoruaimatauea, but Frisbie vigorously disagreed and thought to himself, *Ropati! Think of a frail wisp of a girl dragging a name like that through life! Think of her sweetheart whispering, 'I love you, Ngatoko-ruaimatauea!* The name would never do for him, and thus, he called her Florence after his mother. It would be by her nickname, Whiskey Johnny, or simply, Johnny, that she would be forever known. Still feeling the absence of his first born, Charles, Frisbie vowed to never be separated from Johnny and thereafter the two were seldom apart.

Frisbie felt a strong bond with his oldest daughter the moment she was born. She was precocious and inquisitive and Frisbie thought that she was a real delight. He simply adored her. Throughout the rest of his life Johnny took care of her father, as much as he took care of her. They were dependent upon each other. Later, Johnny would be the author of two volumes of the Frisbie's family reminiscence titled, *Miss Ulysses from Puka-Puka*, published in 1948 and *The Frisbies of the South Seas*, published in 1959.

I first met Johnny Frisbie on Rarotonga on a balmy night in 2002 during a party when the volunteers that I was with were given a feast for our service. I'll never forget it. The feast had the usual fare that consisted of taro, coleslaw, sweet potato, tuna, coconuts, paw-paw and banana. Chicken and pork were cooked in an underground oven called an *umu*. Although the food and festivities were outstanding, the highlight of the night was talking with Johnny, who I learned was the Director/Librarian of the Cook Islands Library and Museum at the time. I have never been one for small talk with other people, but chatting about island life and culture with Johnny and her granddaughter was quite engrossing.

It was a magical evening with star fruit and all. We talked for a couple of hours like two amiable strangers in a cantina. At the time I couldn't believe that I was actually sitting with and speaking to the daughter of Robert Dean Frisbie. I mean, this was the woman who was part of the Frisbie adventure, lore and legends. She grew up on Pukapuka, traveled all over the Pacific Islands. Good Lord, when she was about nine years old she was tied to a tamunu tree on the island of Suwarrow to survive a hurricane. How many people in this world can say they have done that? I told her that I was helping restore the library at the Takitumu School and she thought that it would be a great idea to volunteer at her library. I didn't wait for a second offer and made arrangements to help during the second week of my stay.

Brandon Oswald in Cook Island Library

The Cook Islands Library and Museum was just on the outskirts of the town of Avarua and a short bike ride from where I was staying. I remember showing-up for my first workday at the library dripping with sweat since it was a particularly humid morning. It was normal; it's hard not to sweat in the islands. The library was quaint, well organized and filled to the roof with material. Over the year's benefactors donated most of the books and periodicals that they owned. What really impressed me, however, was the collection of books on the Pacific Islands region. Attached to the library was a museum that added even more ambience to the library.

The museum housed ancient and modern artifacts of the Cook Islands that included an outrigger canoe from Pukapuka and a printing press used by missionaries on Rarotonga. Johnny had me processing paperback books so that they could be ready for circulation. It was a necessary job, but it wasn't a job that required much intellectual thought. *That's okay*, I thought. Sometimes it's nice doing something that's easy and produces low stress. During the day Johnny would make me take a break and walk me around the grounds of the library showing me the different flora that could be found throughout the Cook Islands. She moved very elegantly like an island dance and was very proud of her Polynesian heritage. I kept up with her, perhaps, not as gracefully. Everything had a legend, or a story connected to it. I bet that if I stayed around long enough, a story would have been attached to me.

When I returned home, I kept up a long-distance relationship with Johnny and the Cook Islands Library and Museum. I would donate and send appropriate books and journals for young and old to the library. Sadly, sometime in 2004 I lost touch with Johnny. My only source of communication at the time was through E-mails, and once they dried up, contact was completely lost. After making a couple of attempts to correspond with the Cook Islands Library and Museum staff to see if anyone knew the whereabouts of Johnny, my road came to a dead end as nobody seemed to know where she was living. One person thought that she might have moved to Hawaii. I tried looking for her on the Internet through Facebook pages and websites but to no avail.

It wasn't until eleven years later while doing research for this book that I stumbled upon Johnny's personal E-mail by blindly contacting a person who knew her. One day I was looking at the Cook Islands News online newspaper and saw an article about Amelia Borofsky who lived on Pukapuka when she was a child. At the time she was also helping to raise money to fund a documentary film about herself and Johnny returning to Pukapuka. I quickly dropped everything, found an E-mail for Amelia and sent her a message. I was elated the next day when I received a response containing Johnny's E-mail address and a long-awaited correspondence began again between Johnny and myself. At 83 years old she seemed as lively and passionate about her heritage as ever before. She happened to be very busy at the time preparing to travel back to Pukapuka to shoot the documentary film titled, *Homecoming : A Film About Pukapuka*, and directed by Gemma Cubero del Barrio. This would be an emotional trip for Johnny as she hadn't been back to Pukapuka for several decades. The return would be extra poignant because it would be an opportunity to see her brother, Charles, who she hadn't seen in a long time.

Shortly after Johnny was born, the family sailed the twelve miles from Tahiti to the triangular, rugged and mountainous island of Moorea. Melville had traveled to the island in the 1840s and some of the villages on the eastern coast became models for the Tahitian villages in his novel, *Omoo*, which was published in 1847. Polynesian legend also described the panorama of volcanic ridges as the second dorsal fin of the fish that became the island of Tahiti. These pinnacles later inspired the mythical "Bali Hai" that was based on James

Michener's Pulitzer Prize-winning book, *Tales of the South Pacific.*

James Hall (on left side) and Frisbie in Tahiti

On Moorea, Frisbie decided to try his hand in the poultry business and settled at the head of Paopao Bay. It was an interesting time on this "Garden of Eden" island. Eventually they would add rabbits and goats to the homestead. On long hikes in the island's interior, Frisbie and his wife would discover cool refreshing streams where shrimp would satisfy them as sufficient snacks. Frisbie even made time to collaborate on a book with Charles Nordhoff titled, *Existence Doubtful.* The book was about a soup tureen of pearls hidden on a primitive island. Frisbie wrote to his brother about the book and said, "There is plenty of plot and excitement there, but the principal thing is to show the reader what it was like on an island unknown to whites. I imagine there will be no trouble publishing it." Sadly, he was wrong because the book was never published. In fact, it is unclear if it was ever finished.

One reason that was given for the incomplete novel was that Nordhoff was preoccupied with a concentrated effort towards a South Seas classic that he and Hall were writing together titled, *Mutiny on the Bounty* that would be published by Little Brown and Company. The success of this novel would take the collaborative authors to new heights in the literary world.

In addition to the novel setback with Nordhoff, Frisbie's health made a turn for the worse that made living in paradise very hard. He had a recurrence of filarial fever which plagued him on and off for the rest of his life. Filariasis is a tropical parasitic disease generated by microscopic thread-like worms transmitted by mosquitoes. It causes elephantiasis that leads to engorgement and thickened skin, especially in the limbs. The disease is caused by obstruction of the lymphatic system that results in the accumulation of lymph fluid. It can be treated with the drug, diethylcarbamazine (DEC). Today the disease still affects millions of people in underdeveloped nations, particularly in South America, Africa, Asia, the Caribbean and the Pacific Islands. For Frisbie the disease mainly affected his leg. According to Johnny, her father was able to manage the swelling under a special treatment that consisted of wrapping the leg tightly with bicycle tubing. He also took large doses of quinine to control the disease and kept his activity level to a minimum to help reduce the number of fever outbreaks.

The birth of his second son on October 8, 1933 took Frisbie's health and writing woes off his mind for a short time. The child would be born on the plantation among the hens and rabbits. Frisbie named his son William Hopkins Frisbie, but staying true to his form, created the nickname "Hardpan Jake" for the baby. "Jakey" became the name that stuck.

During the most painful part of the birth of the child, Ngatokorua looked at the jagged mountains of Moorea and saw white terns flying in and out of their caves. This helped keep her mind off the painful delivery. After the birth, she held her son and looked lovingly at him. She told Johnny, "You forget every pain that you ever experienced and wish again to have another baby."

At the time it was becoming quite clear that Frisbie's wife was increasingly becoming more homesick. She also insisted that her next child be born back home on her beloved atoll among her relatives. The plantation was a bust and Frisbie grew weary of his money troubles. He even had to borrow money from his good friend Hall. It was time to leave Tahiti, but alas, they had no money to purchase a ticket on a schooner back to Pukapuka.

Everyone could use a second chance in life and some could even benefit from a third and fourth chance. In January 1934 a chance came to Frisbie to sail a yawl through the Cook Islands that would end at Pukapuka and he did not waste the opportunity to take his wife and children back to the atoll. Although January was a time of year when hurricanes ran rampant in the South Seas, it did not dissuade him from rushing to his family to tell them the fortunate news. They sailed almost immediately and the trip would be quite eventful. Frisbie had bouts with his fever and Ngatokorua was seasick and had a hard time taking care of their two babies. Johnny learned later that she fell overboard and was saved by a sailor named Taiono. When they stopped at the island of Suwarrow that was about two hundred and fifty miles southeast of Pukapuka and five hundred miles east of Samoa, Frisbie's spirits rose. He became intrigued with this desolated place. The island was owned by the A.B. Donald, Ltd. Company who operated a trading post there from time to time.

There was another problem that arose on board ship and continued on the island of Suwarrow. The sailor, Taiono, was throwing amorous affections towards Ngatokorua provoking a fight between him and Frisbie. The inevitable brawl would only be stopped when baby Johnny toddled towards them. Later Taiono apologized and all the trouble was put behind them. As they left Suwarrow, Frisbie was captivated by the thought that the island might make even a better hideaway for a writer than that at Pukapuka. He made a mental note to someday return to this exquisite sanctuary.

Frisbie re-settled with his new family on Pukapuka. It was a nice homecoming for Ngatokorua who now had two children to share among her relatives. Although Frisbie went back to work at the trading station, he desired to spend most of his time with his family on Matauea Point at Ko Islet. It was peaceful and away from

the hustle and bustle of village life. On this islet he could write and live the atoll life again that he once craved. In August of 1934 he wrote to his friend Hall and said, "What a lonely, lost, forgotten place this is! Its detachment from the outside world is sometimes staggering, but it doesn't numb me as it once did. I can sink into the Puka-Puka habit of mind and drift serenely through the days without a thought of anything but food and the life on this microscopic world in itself."

In 1934 Frisbie wrote an article for the *Atlantic Monthly* titled "Cinderella at Puka-Puka" about an event that took place on the atoll. To celebrate the annual May Day festival, each of the three villages performed both a secular and a biblical play. After promising to teach the Windward Village *Cinderella*, Frisbie told them the story. They grasped the spirit of the story, but some of the villagers believed that they could improve it. Frisbie wrote that the Village Fathers held a council and chose a cast that included:

- The Prince: . . . . .Village Dandy George
- Cinderella: . . . . Miss Tern
- Cinderella's Father: . . . . . .Mr. Stomach
- The Fairy Godmother: . . . ,Mrs. Piki-Piki
- Cinderella's Mother: . . . . . Bosun-woman
- Cinderella's Stepmother: . Mrs. Sea Foam
- Village Parson: . . . . .Beni
- The Millionaire's Valet: . . .Deacon Bribery

The play also called for gravediggers, dancers, musicians, soldiers, policemen, a judge and an American Millionaire's yacht. Frisbie could not see how some of these characters fit into the story, but he did not make any objections because he felt that the islanders always had their way of interpreting things.

As they rehearsed, Frisbie noticed mourners crouching over a grave wailing and giggling. Gravediggers stood apathetically to the side while Beni (who played the part of the Village Parson) said prayers. A confused Frisbie then asked, "Beni, what are you doing? There is no burial in Cinderella."

"Hush, Ropati. I'm about to pray," Beni said irritably.

"There are no prayers in Cinderella."

Beni defended the scene again and stated, "We are burying Cinderella's mother. You did not tell us the beginning of the story, but we guessed it. We decided that Cinderella's mother would have to die before her father could marry the widow-woman with two daughters. Of course, there might be a divorce, but that would make two court scenes."

A little later Frisbie heard Beni marrying the American Millionaire to the Stepmother with two daughters. He was intrigued with their perception of the classic story. Frisbie listened to the Millionaire invite the Prince to take part in a great dance at the palace where he will marry the girl who loses her silver slipper at midnight. He then watched the Soldiers march down to the beach and get terribly mixed up trying to do a flank movement whereupon everyone laughed. It was such a good time that they decided to rehearse the scene again.

The rehearsals seemed to take hours. Frisbie came across William, who was watching the entire process with disdain. As Frisbie approached him, William said, "They are having the court scene."

"The what?" Frisbie asked.

"The court scene!" Chief of Police Ura is fining them for dancing after curfew at the Prince's ball."

"Oh, I see," said Frisbie. "I wonder why they don't leave Cinderella out of it altogether and call the play 'Life at Puka-Puka.'"

"That's a great idea," William agreed. "That Cinderella story was about the most foolish thing I ever heard. It's lucky the Puka-Pukans had enough sense to add the death and the burial and the millionaire's yacht and all the other little details."

Frisbie suddenly became aware that one of the world's greatest fairytales was not going to be appreciated by the islanders. He then resignedly said to William, "I guess, there are no Cinderellas on Puka-Puka."

William cantankerously responded, "Hell and Satan! Of course not! All the girls here got their share of the coconuts and the taro whether they have stepmothers or not. And if a girl doesn't like her relations, she doesn't have to live with them. And if she's a good looker, she gets a good man without losing a silver slipper or telling tales to a fat fairy godmother. I will go over to the Village Fathers and advise them to leave Cinderella out of the story." Frisbie would eventually learn that the Village Fathers denied William's request. But they agreed to make Cinderella the Prince's sister and that she would marry the American Millionaire who would start a trading station.

I purposely spent more time describing Frisbie's article, "Cinderella at Puka-Puka" for a couple of reasons. Firstly, I simply thought it was amusing. I wondered what the islanders would have done with great literature classics such as, *Romeo and Juliet* or *Peter Pan*. Nevertheless, it also displayed the mind-set of the islanders and how closely they were tied with their environment and their existence within their village. They showed enthusiasm to learn a new story, but they had to adapt it so that it became relevant in their own world. Although their version of Cinderella seemed farcical, it made more sense to them when they changed the characters and the story to people and situations that they knew. Drama, humor, adventure and romance were mostly brought to life on the atoll by the stories that were orally passed down from generation to generation or what they witnessed in everyday life.

The second reason why I examined the article in more

detail was because it also showed Frisbie's concern with living the carefree island life. By 1934 Frisbie had been on the island for over ten years and his lifestyle was not without strain from several issues. A growing family, a scarcity of ships coming into port, and the judgment of what people in America thought of his decision to live on a lonely atoll were stress factors. In the article Frisbie defended his lifestyle and wrote that he had lived in Pukapuka so long that his acts were governed by feeling and not by reason. He wrote that people who knew him in America thought he was living a futile life. Yet, he retaliated by saying, "I do not feel that it is futile and I do not court regret by reasoning about it; and there is at least the element of surprise which is lacking in orderly existence."

Writing to Hall always seemed to be a kind of therapy for Frisbie; he was never afraid to tell him about his frustrations and worries. Additionally, Hall never hesitated to share positive news. In an exchange of letters, he expressed to his friend that he wished he were there on Pukapuka with him so that they could talk about dreams. "I've been having a dream life such as I've never known before; I long to complete things like novels with definite beginnings and ends," he wrote. In November 1934 Frisbie shared with Hall that his family was living on the uninhabited islet of Ko and that everyone was doing well despite honest poverty. He also proudly noted that Johnny was a very bright and precocious girl, and told Hall that a visiting anthropologist suggested that he should teach her to be bilingual. Frisbie joked that Johnny had learned all the dirty words in Pukapukan and used them indiscriminately before him and his friend, William the Heathen, much to their amusement.

The year of 1935 was an interesting one for Frisbie. He

finished a novel titled *A Child of Tahiti* and believed that, if there were anyone in this world who would like this book, it would be Hall. He wrote to Hall saying that if he should sell anything ever again, he would put every penny towards a cutter that he was building. Frisbie began to dream about sailing himself and his family to Suwarrow Island where he wished to remain for the rest of his life. Also during the same year Johnny noted that her father made another three-week trip to San Francisco. She wrote, "The trip reaffirmed his disillusionment as far as civilization was concerned." Frisbie wrote to his brother bitterly and stated, "By no effort of the imagination will I ever again be able to consider that there are amenities to the life of the gregarious white man." By the end of the year a second daughter, Elaine Metua, was born in Roto Village. According to Johnny who wrote in her book, Miss Ulysses from Puka-Puka, her sister was born so close to midnight that no one was sure if her birthday was the twenty-ninth or the thirtieth of November. They decided on the twenty-ninth due to the fact that the next Frisbie daughter would be born on September 30th a couple of years later, and wanted everyone to have their own special day even to the day of the month.

My Tahiti was published in 1936 by the Little, Brown and Company and was an autobiographical novel of his life on the island. The book consisted of thirty short stories and was not only about the author's time on the island, it was also about how he lived among the Tahitians. The book told how Frisbie invested in property and became a foster child of a native named Tuahu. The stories were charming and witty; the reader got a real sense of what it was like living in Tahiti. It showed how easily Frisbie assimilated into Tahitian society.

The daily life, fishing, adventures with the natives and the interactions with Europeans who drifted in and out of the island were on display throughout the book. The missionaries and Chinese merchants on the other hand were not spared from scorn as Frisbie chastised them for disrupting the easy-going, carefree way of life. The book was full of reminiscences of a time that Frisbie had always looked upon fondly.

Although the publication of *My Tahiti* was a temporary boost to his financial woes, the rest of 1936 truly vexed and exasperated him. A ship had not called into port for over eight months and provisions began to dwindle. Flour, rice and sugar were gone, and Frisbie's diet was simply coconut, fish and taro. Tobacco was nowhere to be found, soap turned to a handful of ashes and his clothes went unwashed. I picture him looking like a shipwrecked Robinson Crusoe. Living without tobacco was really tough on him, so tough that he resourcefully shaved the bowls of

his old pipes and smoked the shavings. In all this time there was no news from the outside world and everyone was becoming a little mad. Every time a child shouted, or a man whooped, everyone was startled into excited tension believing that it was the long awaited, "Sail Ho!"

In June Frisbie wrote to Hall and within this letter one could easily see how the lack of alcohol and tobacco had taken its toll on him. He tells Hall that his children are in good health and that he hoped to take Johnny to Honolulu by the end of the year. Frisbie recognized how his favorite daughter was growing up in a depraved place and that he had had a change of heart in his attitude about the island. "The natural depravity of the Puka-Pukans doesn't interest me anymore; it disgusts me," he scathingly wrote. He goes on to say that he hadn't had any liquor because of his salutary influence of his children including his latest baby daughter, Elaine. He catches his negative tone and writes, "Hall, what kind of letter is this? But remember that my brain is fagged after a long period of intense concentration, and that I have no tobacco." The schooner finally arrived in August and brought much needed supplies. It also brought the bad news that his novel, *A Child of Tahiti*, had been rejected. He pessimistically told Hall that the manuscript that he was currently working on would probably meet the same fate.

Frisbie turned forty-years old in 1937 and his life continued on in the unexpected, carefree way. Although living in the extreme isolation of Pukapuka and the living conditions were quite primitive, Frisbie took great pride for his ability to easily adapt to this harsh lifestyle. He was working on a new novel titled *Javan Moonlight,* which was about a trader living on Pukapuka. He wrote to Hall and told him that the story ran around 150,000 words and he believed it had perfect continuity, a biographical suspense and a "whale of a climax!" Unfortunately, he felt that the novel was too big for him and it had gotten out of hand. Frisbie lamented on not having a critic to keep him on the right track with this piece.

On September 30 Frisbie's last child was born on Matauea Point on Ko Islet. This time his youngest daughter would be given a native name, Ngatokoruaimatauea [Nga-at-Matauea], and Nga for short. In the atolls a name was supposed to be an *akairo*, which is something to remember something by. Nga's Pukapukan name was chosen in reverence to her mother. "Ngatokorua" was used from her mom's name, "I" meant "at," and "Matauea" was the point of land where she was born. Thus her name meant, "In Memory of Mama Ngatokorua at

Matauea." Johnny recalled that Nga was a pretty good troublemaker. Together the two made an excellent pair fighting, racing canoes, screaming and defending themselves against Jakey and Elaine. With the birth of Nga, Frisbie's family would be complete. He would refer to his children as "the cowboys" for the rest of his life, perhaps as homage to the American western frontier and its imperialistic attitude. Despite their trials and tribulations that would plague them in the years to come, Frisbie unequivocally cherished his children and made a solid effort to be a dedicated and caring father.

Frisbie the Writer

CHAPTER
FIVE
THE SPIRIT OF THIS PLACE

How many times has a person heard the Shakespeare quote, "All the world's a stage… …And one man in his time plays many parts…." ("As You Like It," Act II). Indeed, a person's life is a story. It is a novel, a movie or a play. It could be lived as one act, two acts, four acts or as many acts as it takes. As heroes in our own stories, people go through many stages. They endure confrontations, experience ups and downs, encounter plot points and face climaxes. By late 1937 Frisbie was deep into his second act of life and had endured many highs and lows. A major plot point was about to unexpectedly hit Frisbie that would forever change the dynamic of his family and would throw him personally into a world of despair that would take him many years to escape.

Shortly after the birth of Nga, Ngatokorua fell ill with a high fever and had a bad cough. At first Frisbie thought that she had pneumonia or bronchitis, but in the back of his mind he knew it was something more dreadful. He knew what was ailing her, which has been termed the "scourge of the South Seas." It was tuberculosis. The belief that Frisbie himself was the one who, perhaps, inadvertently spread the infectious disease to his wife is debatable. Not many publications about Frisbie approached this topic. In the research article, "White Fathers, Brown Daughter," the author, Elizabeth Deloughrey, stated, "Among the most devastating blows to the Frisbie family romance is the suggestion that Frisbie probably contributed to the death of his own beloved wife. In *Miss Ulysses*, daughter Johnny clearly insinuates that a trading ship brought tuberculosis to Pukapuka and caused her mother's early death from the disease. Johnny's second text, *Frisbies of the South Seas*, revealed that her father brought the illness from the United States. Frisbie wrote extensively about his sick wife, but he never wrote to anyone explaining how his wife contracted the disease.

Although she had good days, her cough persisted. Johnny recalls in her book, *Miss Ulysses from Puka-Puka*, how one day her mother was sweeping the yard and said, "I am happy now, Johnny, because I can work again. I want to work hard every day of my life. It is terrible being sick, for then I cannot work." Sadly, she did not fully recover and very quickly got worse. She continued to cough, spat blood and even had a bad hemorrhage. The family could see that her life was slowly slipping away from her. In January of 1938 Frisbie wrote to his friend and said, "Hall, Nga has tuberculosis and probably won't live longer than a few months. What will I do if she dies? Nga has wasted away to nothing. If she dies I will be left alone with the children. And if I should die...." Years later while writing the book, *The Island of Desire*, Frisbie reflected on this bleak time, questioning the unfortunate luck that seemed to have struck him once again. He wrote:

 I am spending my time trying to escape. Sometimes I wonder if I am spending my life trying to escape from something, myself perhaps. Half my dreams are of running away from an unseen pursuer, leaping down ridges, dashing through forests, swimming across rivers, with the sure knowledge that some person or intangible danger is pursuing me. Never have I seen this pursuer or known what the danger is; but he, or it, is nonetheless terrifying.

It was a very distressing and exasperating time for Frisbie. What could he really do for her? A ship was nowhere in sight. It would take another six months for one to call-in to port. Medicine to ease her suffering was hard to find and Frisbie never trusted native methods of treating illnesses, and even called the native medicine practitioners "witch doctors." Frisbie once described a "witch doctor" treating an islander who had contracted TB in 1928 in an article published by the *Atlantic Monthly* titled, "At Home in Puka-Puka." He wrote, "…he mixes noxious things like fish intestines, chicken droppings, coconut bark, sea urchins and the like for all diseases, external or internal. These he administers in large doses and if the patient is not cured by the power of suggestion he dies from the effect of the medicine." He continued by describing three other methods of treatment. These included, massages for the patient, invocations to the spirits of the dead who cause the patient's illness by possessing his body, and placing the patient on a strict diet of a very coarse kind of taro, land crabs and coconut crabs.

The British warship, H.M.S. *Leith*, called in at Pukapuka in June 1938. It was nice to finally get a ship in port but it was not the trading schooner that Frisbie and his family had hoped for that would bring nourishing food, or could take Ngatokorua to a hospital. Johnny recalls her mother telling her, "Johnny, my dear! Pray for a ship! I want to go away and get well! I want to live so I can see my babies grow up! Pray for a ship Johnny! Pray for a ship!" Despite the fact that his wife was getting worse, Frisbie continued to work on scripts. He was constantly pecking away at his typewriter throughout the day and night. The typing helped to drown-out the sounds of her coughing. Focusing solely and getting lost in a novel or an article also helped take his mind off his ailing wife.

Frisbie could not wait for another ship any longer and decided to go aboard the *Leith* with the resident agent to seek the ship's doctor. Although the British warship was about to sail, the doctor was persuaded to quickly go to Frisbie's wife who was at the trading station. During the examination the doctor listened to her chest, tapped it and told her to say, "ninety-nine, ninety-nine...." As usual, onlookers filled the windows and doorway like troublesome birds until Frisbie chased them off. The doctor believed that Ngatokorua had TB and took Frisbie over to a house where the *Leith*'s captain and other officers were having tea. The doctor told the captain that Frisbie's wife would die if she were not taken to the hospital in Samoa. At the time there was a strict rule to not allow women aboard a British warship but the captain eventually acquiesced. Frisbie and his son Jakey accompanied

Ngatokorua to help nurse her on the voyage to Apia. The girls would remain behind on Pukapuka with relatives.

Worrying about his wife soon took its toll on Frisbie during their stay in Samoa. He wrote to Hall in October that loneliness drove him to trouble as he went on a drinking spree, got thrown into jail and the next day was fined a pound for inciting a riot. He also mentioned that although he did not receive a single cent from any manuscripts, he did receive eight $50 Government checks that he had to turn over to the administration as a deposit for his wife's hospitalization. "Jakey and I are without a bean and more or less living on charity," he told Hall.

After several days of treatment, Frisbie's optimism seemed to rise regarding his wife's health and he believed that there was some chance for her to live. He noted that Ngatokorua was undergoing what was called a pneumothorax treatment. The goal of this treatment was to relieve the pressure on the lungs and allow them to re-expand. Frisbie commented that the treatment was long, tedious and often painful, but was worth the undertaking because of its success rate. He noted that patients that suffered from the disease worse than her had been cured by the treatment. The doctors estimated that the treatment could take over a year to rehabilitate her, and that forced Frisbie to state, "I'll be head over heels in debt, but what of it? I'll do what Governments of England, France and the rest do. I'll borrow money with no intentions to pay it back."

The Frisbie boys tried their best to pass the time in Samoa waiting for news from the doctors on whether or not Ngatokorua would live. Both would visit her in the hospital but the visits were usually short because of her condition.

They could do little more than look at her. Hall noted that Frisbie's resolve to stay sober was not adhered to which was understandable considering the situation. Frisbie and Jakey tried to stay active by taking long walks in the country. Jakey would later tell his sisters about his adventures in Samoa where he rode in motorcars, on horseback and ate ice cream. Frisbie got a chance to visit Vailima, which was the former house of Robert Louis Stevenson and now was the home of the Resident Commissioner of Western Samoa. Frisbie could not help but compare the circumstances of the world-famous, tubercular Stevenson to those of himself, the penniless author of many rejected manuscripts and husband of a tubercular wife.

In late 1938 Frisbie got news that the doctors wanted to talk about his wife's condition at the hospital. It was the news that he dreaded but inevitably was waiting for him. The doctors told him that Ngatokorua's treatment had gone wrong, that she was in critical condition and might die at any moment. They were keeping her alive with the bitter alkaloid, strychnine, which was also used medicinally as a stimulant for the central nervous system. She was also given digitalis drugs that was made from a type of foxglove plant and used to produce a stimulating effect on the heart. At night morphine was provided to help her sleep. Knowing that the boat, *Matafele*, was sailing to Pukapuka around Christmas, Frisbie insisted on taking his wife back to her home despite the doctors' grim prediction that she would die before they reached the atoll. They left anyway and made it back home where her relatives and children could share her last few weeks on earth.

Ngatokorua died on January 14, 1939. Before she passed

away, she spoke to Frisbie one last time and said, "Keep all my children, Ropati. Give none of my children to the relatives. Promise me, Ropati that you will keep all my children and love them and bring them up like white children." She then mustered all her energy to tell her children to stay with their father, love him and obey him. She continued faintly and warned her children that people would try to take them away from their father, but do not listen to them. Frisbie told Hall in a letter that when the end became very near, he sat on the floor with his back against one of the roof-posts with his wife in his arms. Her position in his arms reminded him of when he held her in the same way the year before when they were alone on Ko Islet and their last baby was born. Then there was a convulsive shudder and her breathing stopped and she fell limp in his arms. He held her for about a half-hour, then he closed her eyes, bathed, clothed and kissed her goodbye. Neighbors and relatives then took the body away and Frisbie would never see her again.

The death ceremony would have been excruciating for Frisbie to endure. Polynesians believed in life after death and the wall between the living and the dead is more permeable than in a modern Western culture. When a person is about to die, or has died, family and friends must establish methods for both detachment and attachment from the living world. Throughout all of Polynesia and in parts of Melanesia, the troublesome presence of a dead person reveals the existence of unfinished business that must be resolved before the soul can depart in peace. In New Zealand, for example, the Maoris trampled through the house to reclaim it for the living. Chants, dirges and poetic lamentations would also commence as soon as a person dies. In Hawaii wailers would come to a wake and offer chants called *kanikau* for the deceased that were deeply about the dead person's life and the connections to others. On the Fijian island of Rotuma wailing would begin at the moment a person dies asking inane questions such as, "Why are you leaving us so soon?" or "Why did you have to go?"

Frisbie experienced the death chants on Pukapuka numerous times, but he never forgot one that occurred to his friend Wail-of-Woe who died from tuberculosis during the first few years of living on the island. He captured the death in writing in his 1928 article publication, "At Home in Puka-Puka." He remembered, "Screech after screech cut through the still night air, but at length these subsided and the death chant burst forth." He struggled to describe such a sound because he had nothing to compare it to in a modern civilization. "The sounds range from eerie guttural moans rising slowly to ear-splitting screams when the wife throws her body across the dead husband and tearing her hair with outcries that chill the blood." When Frisbie first heard one of these songs, he was fascinated by its unearthly, eerie quality and oddly found himself unconsciously swaying his body in unison with the meaningless syllables of the unchanging cadence. Frisbie noted that the relatives exhausted themselves emotionally as the death chants for Wail-of-Woe lasted all that night and the next day and night.

Frisbie would have refrained from participating in any formal church memorial service for his wife given his history of traveling around during his youth with his father who looked for a faith to attach the family to. That experience made Frisbie distrust religions. Unfortunately for him, moving to the South Seas did not rid himself of preaching evangelists. Missionaries had already swarmed the ports throughout all of the islands in the region. After his first five years in Tahiti, he wrote a scathing letter to his brother in 1925 stating:

 Missionaries in the South Seas, brother, are a fizzle. The natives are much more Godly without them. The imbeciles come down here and first of all break down the old customs, thereby creating such ennui that the natives have to join the churches to pass the time. The missionaries forbid dancing and native himene singing, and heathen rites, thereby leaving nothing for the natives to do for a pastime. Hence the church is the only outlet for their spare energy. Of course the damn missionaries are quite aware of the fact that they are forcing the natives into church by taking away all their amusement... they have actually taught the natives sins so as to have something to forgive.

Frisbie was not the only South Seas writer to complain about the missionaries. Herman Melville spent time in Hawaii, Marquesas and Tahiti where he witnessed the missionary efforts among the islanders. The religious conversion of the Polynesian natives led him to question the missionaries' activities. Melville truly felt that the islanders would have been better off left to their own devices as opposed to being converted to the Euro-American standards of civilized living. He once dramatically wrote that instead of receiving the benefits of Christian living, the natives were reduced to a devastating and dehumanized existence and were being driven to a cultural death.

Like Melville, Robert Louis Stevenson was quite critical of the work that missionaries were doing in the Pacific Islands. He wrote off Christian missions as having a dire effect on islanders. Stevenson changed his tune, however, in his later years as he got to know several missionaries while living in Samoa. He even recorded, "Those who have a taste for hearing missions, Protestant or Catholic, decried, must seek their pleasure somewhere else than in my pages. Whether Catholic or Protestant... with all their deficiency... the missionaries are the best and the most useful whites in the Pacific."

If there were one phrase that best described the missionaries in the Pacific region, it would be: "the great resolve." It was not very long after the death of Captain James Cook that the first ship, *The Duff,* made its way to Tahiti carrying lower-middle-class Protestant clergymen, lay preachers and tradesmen from the London Missionary Society (LMS). The ship reached Matavai Bay in March 1797 where they built their church and established a little colony. The missionaries had little interest in anthropology or Tahitian customs and were also indifferent for any kind of scientific discoveries. They were practical workers in the cause of the Lord and wanted to change the island in the image of their lower-middle-class Protestant England. Despite not knowing the language, withstanding tropical diseases and facing unpredictable behavior from the islanders, their success was actually quite astonishing. The missionaries never dismayed or turned away from their purpose. Persistently and firmly they pummeled away like a chisel on stone at the Tahitian way of life and achieved their goal within two decades. The timing was perfect for missionaries to suppress the heathenism of the island as at the time the Tahitians were deemed as lazy, un-resistant and wanted to imitate the manners of the western world. The clergyman and the tradesman looked like kids with new ideas and toys and the Tahitians wanted to play like them.

The pattern for converting the Polynesians quickly emerged after the landing of *The Duff*. Once they overcame the initial hardships and resistance, they learned the language and then went straight to the top and converted the chief. They knew that the reluctance to give up their idols would be severely weakened once the paramount leader had denounced his ancient religious beliefs. The Reverend John Williams, who was perhaps one of the most famous and enterprising of the LMS missionaries in the Society Islands, added a third very important step in the conversion, which was to have trained islanders preach the Gospel.

From the beginning of the LMS, Williams knew that there were an insufficient number of clergymen to spread the Gospel to other islands in the region. He created a way to recruit and train Polynesian teachers whom he felt could establish contact with their own or related peoples. New converts were urged to augment mission funds with contributions of saleable goods and money. Thus, each Polynesian church was given a definite stake in the overseas activity of the mission. It was under this scheme that the missionaries arrived in the southern Cook Islands in 1821. Williams first landed two preachers on the island of Aitutaki, and from there, they eventually branched out to other islands including Rarotonga. It was an inventive plan that worked. Williams dedicated most of his life evangelizing throughout the region. On the island of Erromango in the New Hebrides (now Vanuatu) his calling would come to end as he was clubbed to death and eaten by cannibals in 1839.

Although the missionaries were responsible for the negative aspects of life, including the destruction of culture throughout Oceania, there were some remarkable men among them that meant nothing but good and actually made some positive advancements within the islands. For example, the missionaries were the ones who created schools and wrote down the language. They also had a huge impact on the land, structure of society and the people. Some Oceania historians believed that the missionaries influenced the traditional gender roles of Pacific Islands' women by treating them as equal with the island men. Throughout the latter part of the 19th century less importance was put on authority figures being solely male and some women became influential in the public realm. One last crucial change that missionaries effected was the way in which the islanders were governed. A centralized form of government under elected politicians gradually replaced the traditional tribal system where hereditary chiefs were in control. This also affected the concept of a cash economy that replaced the traditional barter system.

The missionaries did not arrive on Pukapuka until 1857 when the LMS landed two teachers from the islands of Aitutaki and Rarotonga. Some of the villagers wanted to kill the newcomers for the disrespect of their idols but were spared when a chief intervened and protected the preaching men. By 1862 most of people on the island had converted to Christianity. Today Pukapukans remain very religious with the largest denomination being Cook Islands Congregationalist (derived from the former London Missionary Society). A smaller percentage of islanders are Catholic and Seventh-Day Adventists. All three groups practice a conservative form of Christianity in which the Sabbath is strictly observed.

Johnny recalls that the Sabbath on the island was a colorful day and enjoyed watching all the islanders show-off their Sunday finest. This usually meant that they were dressed in white calico dresses or white pants. The fun of it was to see how many of these fancy dressers got through the morning without smudging their outfits from the unpredictable island environment. She also remembered how her father shied away from going to Sunday services, however, he did believe in God. In fact, he enjoyed reading the Bible and taught his children the Twenty-third Psalm. Frisbie just simply believed that one did not need to go to church and that one could worship God while alone in a room, even naked or dressed. He once told his daughter, "A lot of people go to church to show their new dresses; some even go to worship. But people don't know that they can reach God anywhere." Johnny was unsure about her father's stance on religion. She thought that the many authors he read during his nightly reading heavily influenced him. Johnny could not help but feel very sinful for not attending church that often, but her father reminded her by stating, "If you believe sincerely in your prayers you need not go to church, and you need not worry about God ignoring you, for it isn't true that he would! That is not in his character."

On Sundays the sidewalks roll-up throughout all of the Pacific Islands as commercial establishments are closed; the streets are empty. The cacophony of sounds that usually come from the markets are still as most islanders are at church. If the founding missionaries could see their work today, they would have a smile on their face. Those who died horribly by disease and cannibals would feel that it was all worth it. As a

South Seas traveler and a Catholic myself, I too wonder how much culture has been lost at the hands of the missionaries. I do my best to try to think more about the positive outcomes that were brought on from the conversion. I don't stay away from attending mass on Sunday. On the contrary, I look forward to going to a service, if for anything, to listen to the singing.

I remember attending my first Pacific Islands mass at St. Joseph's Cathedral in Avarua during that first volunteer trip to the island of Rarotonga, Cook Islands. Outside the weather was ominous, as thick dark clouds threatened rain. Inside it was balmy and the atmosphere was oppressive. Everyone waited in hopeful anticipation for the clouds to break with rain and relieve us from the heaviness of the air. While waiting for mass to start, I recall wondering if I was overdressed or underdressed for the service. It was hard to tell in my Hawaiian shirt. But, one thing I did know was that I was hot and sweaty and was desperate to keep moving. Sitting still in the middle of a pew with nowhere to go, I got a little claustrophobic. I was dying. Then the singing began, unbelievable singing, like a choir of angels, and I was immediately transferred to another world. Outside streams of sunlight broke through the clouds creating this exquisite, holy and ethereal experience. I don't know what it was. Perhaps, it was the timbre of Pacific Islander voices that I wasn't used to hearing in the Western part of the world that truly impressed me. The singing was purely angelic. All of a sudden I wasn't hot or sweaty or dying. It didn't matter to me if I was naked or dressed in fancy clothes. I was simply transcended peacefully and without a care in the world.

After the death of his wife, Pukapuka lost its charm for

Frisbie. He found it hard to find inspiration; the island was no longer a beautiful, ideal place for writing and raising his children. He confided in Hall that he was fed up with Pukapuka and that he had confused his love of Ngatokorua with love for the island. "With her death it has lost every atom of its glamour. Even Matauea Point, that I used to think a paradise, is now nothing but an uninteresting sand-bank." Frisbie was broke again but it did not deter him from writing. In the back of his mind Suwarrow Island beckoned and would become his new muse. He dreamed of ways of getting there. In the meantime, he became even more critical about his writing. He wanted to be so good the critics would rave about him. The thought of not succeeding brought out other worries. He wrote, "Twenty years of writing without success, the one romance of my life ended, and my children: what will become of them if anything happens to me."

Frisbie could have easily given his "cowboys" to relatives and loosen the burden of raising them. But, he took his wife's dying request to heart, plus he truly loved his cowboys. When the idea that he would not be able to raise the children fluttered around the atoll, he stubbornly disagreed. Frisbie famously wrote a passage to Hall that would be utilized in many research papers about him:

> I failed to see why a man cannot bring up children as well as a woman can, and now, after seven months' experience, I know that he can. All this 'only a mother knows' is rubbish. A man is quite as capable as a woman, though usually he is too lazy to take on the job. He is not apt to spoil

his children by sloppy sentiment. He makes them self-reliant.

Hall stated that the dread of dying while his children were still alive became a kind of obsession with Frisbie. This fear would come up from time to time in subsequent letters that Frisbie wrote to Hall.

For a few years Frisbie was working on a novel titled *Javan Moonlight*. Draft after draft the project became a labor of love and he had a grandiose idea for the book. He wanted it to be a trilogy, perhaps inspired by Hall and Nordhoff's Bounty saga. Frisbie wrote to Hall telling him that the trilogy would be made up as: Volume 1: *The Genesis of a Recluse*; Volume 2: *The Saga of William the Heathen*, and; Volume 3: *The Revelations of a Recluse* Knowing the success that the *Mutiny on the Bounty* had had as a movie, Frisbie dreamed that once his *Javan Moonlight* trilogy was finished, it too, would be sold to the movies. The thought of the possibility of financial success must have eased his mind for a short time. Sadly, in the same letter he questioned and doubted his dream. He wrote, "*The Saga of William the Heathen* could be filmed if I can keep from spoiling it with too much introspective musing. But the other two not a hope."

In late 1939 the first (and only) volume of the trilogy was published by Farrar & Rinehart, and was re-titled *Mr. Moonlight's Island*. Hall was never truly impressed by the novel because it used many characters and scenes from the *Book of Puka-Puka*. Hall's assessment of the novel was backed-up by *The Saturday Review*. The review read as if it was taking a passage straight from Frisbie's classic 1929 *The Book of Puka-Puka*: Javan

Moonlight, manager of the Line Islands Trading Company's station at Danger Island, is not a transient looking with wide eyes at the curious customs of the natives, to return to civilization and write a book about his experiences; he is a fixture and as such a part of the life around him. Observer, philosopher, interpreter, he also lives as a member of the community. Today, *Mr. Moonlight's Island* remains one of Frisbie's hardest to find novels. If one does find a rare copy of the book, it will most likely cost the person an arm and a leg to purchase it.

The death of his wife continued to take its toll on Frisbie. Relatives incessantly bickered over the children and believed that Frisbie should distribute them in the native tradition. Johnny recalls that her father was also not right in the head. When he was writing, he would suddenly stop, and shout, "Johnny, run and ask Mama to make me a pot of tea!" Or, when they sat down for dinner, Frisbie would ask where their mother was and the children would tell him that she had gone to the *motu* for a few days. At night in bed he would talk to his wife as if she were lying next to him, telling her his troubles and his plans. He yearned of buying a ship and sailing her all over the world. He wrote Hall that he felt as if he was losing contact with the Faustian culture and entering into the Magian culture of Pukapuka. He said, "I find myself continually thinking in Puka-Pukan, and it requires an effort to shift back to English. When a man thinks in a new language he enters the culture of that language." Frisbie knew that it was time for him to leave the atoll and wondered if it would be possible for him to live anywhere else than Pukapuka. He decided to find out and chose Fiji as his first destination.

Frisbie decided to take his daughter Johnny and another Pukapukan named Araipu. He was the branch storekeeper as well as the vicar of the London Missionary Service church to Fiji. It was an odd trio but they grew to be dependent upon each other during their time abroad. They sailed on the *Tagua*, which at the time was being used to carry lepers from Penrhyn to the leper colony at Makogai, Fiji. When the adventure began, Frisbie had dreams of being a peddler much like the ones he remembered in California who made their rounds selling their goods twice a year. The way these peddlers slept and cooked in their covered wagons impressed him. This inspired him to get a boat and do the same. He imagined himself stocking up in Sydney, Suva or Singapore and then wandering all over the Pacific selling his wares. "And think of the literary material I'll gather along with the profits of trading," he enthusiastically wrote to Hall. "*The Saga of a South Sea Peddler*—the book is as good as written and I don't see how it could fail to be accepted." Frisbie hoped Farrar & Rinehart and the *Atlantic Monthly* would advance him $2,500 for future work so that he could buy a boat that would be converted to a sea-peddler by Araipu and himself. He believed that Araipu was shrewd enough to be a good supercargo while he played the role as captain and navigator. As for his children, he would base his headquarters at Suwarrow Island. He would leave his children to be looked after by William the Heathen and his wife, Old Mama.

The trio toured all over the main island of Viti Levu and even spent about four months in the main town of Suva. Fiji was a very different world than Pukapuka. For one thing, Fijians are not Polynesians like the people from the Cook Islands. They are Melanesian and much darker in complexion with black, frizzy hair. Fiji is also the only Pacific Island that is multiethnic. A large population of Indo-Fijian (From India) with their unique blend of beliefs and customs live throughout the islands.

When Fiji became a British Crown Colony in 1847, the British recruited mostly young illiterate farmers from villages across India to come to Fiji to work in the cane fields and sugar mills. The recruited workers were known as indentured laborers and when they got to their adopted new country, they thrived. By the end of their contracts, these independent Indian farmers began leasing land to earn a living in sugar cane, cotton, tobacco and rice cultivation. In 1919 the use of indentured servants was abolished and Indians were given the chance to go home or stay in the islands. Most stayed and became diversified even further by becoming shopkeepers, clerks, public servants and domestic help. By the time Frisbie arrived in Suva in the early 1940s, the Indo-Fijians outnumbered the indigenous Fijians.

Today, Fiji's census shows that Indigenous Fijians account for about 51 percent of the population while Indo-Fijians are at about 43 percent. For the most part, the two groups live in peace and harmony. There were some race relation difficulties in the mid-1970s shortly after independence from Britain, and occasionally, cultural differences between the two groups have proven rich fodder for political agitations. But, a century of living together has definitely had a profound effect on both groups as they interact culturally and participate in each other's festivals, sporting games, places of worship and the workplace.

Since I have had many volunteer projects in Suva over the past few years, I can verify the harmony in the workplace between the indigenous and the Indo-Fijians. I worked in places such as the University of South Pacific and the National

Archives where the staff was composed of a mix of Indo-Fijians and indigenous Fijians. Both groups were very easy to get along with, and because of their engaging and social characteristics, projects were completed without any issues. Workplace feasts at the end of a project were unforgettable as I got to eat not only indigenous Fijian cuisine, but I also got to try favorite traditional Indian fare. I think my favorite observation was how the Indo-Fijians have mostly done away with the rigidities of India's caste and social structure. Instead, they have adopted a more laid-back Melanesian way of life.

During their stay in Fiji, Frisbie continued to teach Johnny her lessons every day, even on Sundays. On nice days the two would take long walks where his daughter would recite her multiplication tables. Johnny remembered how much fun it was writing and drawing in the sand. During their time outdoors it was the environment that Frisbie wanted Johnny to become aware of. He wanted her to feel the familiar spirit of place. Every South Seas writer noticed it, experienced it, lived it and wrote about it. Frisbie would tell Johnny to use all her senses and to smell the place, hear the sounds and to taste the food in the different restaurants—the familiar spirit of place. Johnny wrote that they would take the time to listen to the "singsong speech" of the Chinese, the high-pitched, excited jabber of the Indians, the screaming of the children in the street, the tapping of the shoemakers' mallets, the jewelers' hammers and the noise of traffic. At the same time the two would smell the spicy odors from the Indian shops, the appetizing ones from the Chinese restaurants and the smell of fish and meat at the market. "Listen, and look and smell at the same time," Frisbie would say to his daughter. "Then let your mind go blank and you will feel the spirit of this place."

Nobody captured the spirit of a place like South Seas writers and Johnny would one day do the same when writing her own books.

It was an exciting time to be in Fiji as it was the outbreak of World War II and everyone was on high alert. Many soldiers were in Suva during this time. Johnny wrote that enemy raiders

were in the Pacific. Ships were being sunk, mines were being laid in the harbors and islands were being shelled. Planes roared above the town every day and everybody was expecting the Japanese at any time. Despite the threat of the war washing upon Fiji's shores, it did not deter Frisbie and his small entourage from traveling around the island.

They started their around-the-island adventure on December 31, 1940 and visited other towns and villages. One of the first stops was at the small island of Bau where Raku Cakobau once lived and reigned. Cakobau was born around 1815 and was credited as the king who united some of Fiji's warring tribes, establishing a united Fijian Kingdom. He was a giant of a man and terrifying in his heathen days. Legend has it that he had killed and eaten 1000 bodies before his conversion to Christianity. Before his death in 1883, he ceded the Fijian islands to the United Kingdom with the hope that British rule would bring civilization, as well as Christianity, throughout all of Fiji.

Overall, the trip to Fiji did not go as well as Frisbie had hoped. His plans of buying a boat for his sea-peddling dream did not materialize and Farrar & Rinehart and the *Atlantic Monthly* turned down his request for advanced money. Disillusioned, he wrote to Hall and said, "I suppose if I had asked for an advance to go to the war zone to report gruesome details of wholesale murder, I could have gotten all the cash I wanted." The money that he and Araipu had was gone and he thought about his children that he left on Pukapuka, wondering when he would see them again. He continued to lament to Hall, "As you have sometimes, and eloquently said: I am bitched, bewitched, blighted and bewildered. What in particular has bewitched me has been my own foolishness. I am always too hopeful." Frisbie often went to Suva to look for something to keep his mind off his troubles. Johnny recalled that she would sometimes pedal her bicycle from one place to another looking for him. When she found him, she would take him home. The three knew that their sojourn in Fiji was coming to an end and that it was time to return to Pukapuka.

As luck would have it, Frisbie, Johnny and Araipu were able to book passage on the luxury liner *Monterey* that would take them to Pago Pago, Samoa. Johnny was in awe of the ship, as she had never seen anything like it. The ship had lounges, ping-pong tables, picture shows, a swimming pool, tennis court, masquerade balls, elevators, and pretty lady passengers. When they arrived in Pago Pago, it was full of marines, sailors, contractors, and thousands of native laborers. Johnny also noticed that the docks were crowded with antiaircraft guns, canons, trucks, tanks and munitions. "Uncle Sam was fortifying his islands. As everybody in the South Seas knew, the United States would soon be in the war," she said. It would take another nine months, or so, when the "sleeping giant" was officially forced into the war after the attack on Pearl Harbor in Hawaii by the Japanese.

Frisbie and his small group did not stay in Pago Pago for very long. Five days later they sailed to Apia, Western Samoa on the coasting schooner, *Amy*. In Apia they lived off the land for three months waiting for a ship to take them to Pukapuka. They eventually boarded the cutter *Taipi* and sailed the four hundred miles in very squally weather. It would take the ship three weeks to reach Pukapuka. Frisbie felt more at home on this tiny boat and preferred it to the luxury liner. He would play cards with the captain every day and the two became good friends. The captain, who was a teetotaler, even tried to persuade Frisbie to sign a pledge to not drink anymore. Frisbie told the captain that he would think about it, but he never committed to it.

Johnny recalled that upon their return home the first thing that the Pukapukans wanted to learn were the songs, dances and games that she learned while in Fiji. This was a normal practice since ancient times for natives of the South Seas, as songs and dances are very much imbedded into their culture. For weeks Johnny taught them all kinds of new lyrics and dance moves, especially the famous Fiji song, "Isa Lei," which was (and still is) a Fiji farewell song. Many tourists may have heard the "Isa Lei" on the last day of their stay at a Fijian resort. Melodic and inspiring, its sweet notes rise in layers of hymn-like stanzas. I, personally, love the "Isa Lei." It is haunting, yet beautiful. Whenever I attend a conference in the Pacific Islands, many islanders from all over the region would join me. On the last day of the conference the attendees would usually breakout in song and sing the "Isa Lei." It didn't matter which island you were from, you knew how to sing the Fijian song. For the first couple of conferences that I attended, I didn't know the lyrics, so I did my best to hum along. Today I can get by with a few verses.

As Johnny was telling her siblings, relatives and friends all about her faraway adventures, Frisbie settled back down on

Pukapuka. For him the Fiji experience was not a happy one and being back on the atoll was difficult as the remembrance of his wife was found everywhere. He often fell into reflective and meditative thought and tried doing activities that were conducive to contemplation. While sitting on the point at Yato, he wrote to Hall and described one of these daydreams:

> I was in harmony with my surroundings. I stared across the crescent-shaped bay to the main islet. A few houses on the far beach were white in the evening sunlight, but farther back in the groves they were scarcely visible. The deep shadows suggested sleep, as did the coconut palms. These last held their fronds silent and still, in deep dreamless sleep; but when a faint breeze passed over them, whispering some dream image, the fronds stirred slightly in their sleep, then rested once more as the image passed away. The dreaming palms have escaped awareness of life.

In the same letter Frisbie tried to once again justify his lifestyle on Pukapuka to his best friend. He wrote that even though he was still poor, he still ate, slept under a roof and had an occasional bottle of mangaro beer. He even bragged that he had many servants such as, a washerwoman, cooks, fishermen (for when he was too lazy to fish for himself), food-gatherers, and even had his own private storyteller and comedian in William the Heathen. Although he was once again proud of his idyllic life on the atoll, he was restless and yearned for travel. He wanted to take his four cowboys on a lengthy cruise among the islands of the South Seas. Preparations for the voyage commenced and the family left Pukapuka shortly after Christmas in 1941 on the *Taipi*, which Frisbie called a sea-house that just barely managed to keep afloat. The first stop on their adventure would be at the uninhabited island known as Suwarrow. Finally, Frisbie made it back to the unspoiled paradise that gave him happy memories of the three months he spent there with his wife. He described Suwarrow as the loveliest, loneliest atoll in the Pacific and had dreamed to make it an enduring home for him and his family.

Suwarrow was an uninhabited, low-lying coral atoll and consisted of many small islets on a barrier reef that enclosed a large lagoon. There was only one small anchorage off the appropriately named islet, Anchorage Island. When the Russian ship, *Suvorov*, landed in 1814, the crew found nobody living on the island. They named the island after the ship's name, Alexander Suvorov, who was a Russian general. Suwarrow became the official spelling that was adopted by New Zealand.

During the cruise of the *Janet Nichol* in 1890 Fanny Stevenson described the island as "the most romantic island in the world." Although her husband had published *Treasure Island* some years prior to their visit, he would have agreed on Suwarrow's other name, which was Treasure Island. The interior of the island was covered with a tangled, dense tropical foliage. It was thickly populated by many varieties of sea birds and when they were disturbed, they made a deafening cacophony of noise like members of an orchestra tuning their instruments at the same time. The lagoon was dotted with small islets encircling the reef that was teeming with fish. In addition to the plethora of birds living on the island, there were other forms of wild life in abundance as well. Johnny stated that land crabs scurried this way and that, hermit crabs and golden-green lizards crawled and leaped among the branches, centipedes wriggled in the piles of rubbish and huge coconut crabs would rear back with their claws spread out.

Intriguingly, Suwarrow had a dark side too. The trader, Tom Richards, believed the reason the island was uninhabited was because of its "gruesome history." Evil spirits of murdered people reportedly haunted it. He claimed, "Many ships had been wrecked upon Suwarrow and the ghosts of their crews walked the night." Richards also believed the haunting reports created by superstitious natives who had lived on the island from time to time were true. He also had no trouble accepting the statements from white overseers who swore the island was haunted.

In his book *White Man, Brown Woman,* Richards asserted that the spirits of the dead walked the night on Suwarrow. He wrote that many of the dead who perished in their ships near the island would walk the beach at night. Richards would tell the story about a treasure hunter named George Randolph, who led a treasure-hunting expedition to Suwarrow. Before he sailed to the island, Randolph went to the island of Penrhyn. While there, he acquired several hundred laborers to bring to Suwarrow to help him unearth the treasure. For several weeks they worked in the hot sun but could not find any coins.

Chaos and unrest soon followed, and the islanders began to complain about ghosts appearing at night from an old wreck on the reef. Laborers started dying from illness; the survivors connected the deaths with the ghosts. Randolph knew the spirits would affect the morale and subsequently the work of the laborers. He spent many nights sitting on the beach watching for apparitions. On one such a night, he saw something peculiar and wrote in his diary, "I think I'm slowly going mad. Last night I saw ghosts on the reef. They wore large hats with great feathers and short baggy trousers with leggings." Randolph told his crew he planned to set the wreck on fire in the hope that it would help the remaining laborers to go back to work, but they became fearful that this move would only make the spirits angrier. Fearing retribution from the spirits for his plan, the laborers locked Randolph in the gunpowder shed and set fire to it. They then sailed away and the island was deserted again for many years.

The belief in ghosts in Polynesian culture was quite widespread and continues to this day. Many Polynesians believe that after a person dies, some ghosts travel to either the sky world or the underworld, while others stay on earth. Often, ghosts were reported to be actively involved with the affairs of the living. In his 1990 paper, "That Isn't Really a Pig: Spirit Traditions in the Southern Cook Islands," Christian Clerk examined the oral tradition of ghost stories in the Cook Islands. He wrote extensively about the *tupapaku*—spiritual beings or forces who became detached from the body after a human or animal was gone. According to legend, these spirits would wander the island until they reached their final underworld destination called *te Po*. *Tupapaku* could be dangerous; stories about death, disease and misfortune associated with spirit contact, very much like the one about the treasure hunter on Suwarrow that Richards told, perpetuated fear in those who visited the island.

Frisbie and his cowboys were also aware of the shadowy history of the island, especially the shipwrecks that had created so many legends. Even before they arrived, the shipwrecks were noted in visitor's diaries. In May of 1890 Fanny Stevenson would log in her journal what she saw in one of the single-room houses on the island. She said that piled in one corner of the house was a treasure-trove from vessels that had been wrecked on Suwarrow and included such items as, a ship's blocks and sails, antiquated firearms, iron parts, tool chests, steering-wheels, harpoons and life-preservers. Always inquisitive, the Frisbies were constantly on the hunt for lost artifacts. They found human bones and a headstone and wondered and tried to discover treasure hidden beneath the coral. Nevertheless, the nights were eerie and the group never slept far apart. Years later it was only natural for Frisbie to draw upon his time on Suwarrow when he was writing his novel, *Amaru*.

The family settled on the islet of Anchorage Island, which was the largest of the islets on Suwarrow. Frisbie described the island as a gloom-haunted mass of low-lying jungle less than a mile long. In the book *The Island of Desire* Frisbie wrote how the island was alive with memories of men who had lived in her fastness, had dug gold, weighed pearls, loved native women, caroused, fought and died. He then added, "Now time and the jungle had claimed Suwarrow; now the creeping and flying creatures had returned to the fastness; now only memories of the old days remained."

They utilized a stone wharf and an old trading post that was once used when the island was on the trading map. When they arrived, the trading post was in severe decay. Frisbie and his children would use the lumber from the post to build a house among the branches of one of the giant *tamanu* trees. Frisbie wrote to Hall and characterized how the children stayed busy. He told his friend that they fished from the fringes of reef, swam in the lagoon, hunted sea birds on the sand cays and stalked turtles and coconut crabs. They never hesitated visiting the other islets in their canoe, *Panikiniki* (Skipping Stone), which they brought with them. These frequent trips opened up new possibilities and adventures. They would spend the night on the islets and Frisbie once confided with Hall that the place was so lonely that, for the first time in his life, he felt a touch of panic at the extreme isolation.

Although it was a great time for the cowboys to go native, Frisbie only allowed them to be happy "savages" for half the time. Johnny recalled that every morning her siblings and she had to wash their face, comb their hair, brush their teeth and after breakfast t they had to wash and put away dishes and other items used for the meal. Then they had to do the thing that all children worldwide dreaded, schoolwork. Johnny once lamented that they, "Study, for hours at a stretch, stupid schoolbooks, when all about us lay Suwarrow Atoll, adventure such as we never again could hope to enjoy!"

After a few weeks of exploring the islets that were devoid of human beings, Frisbie's island was invaded much to his chagrin. A cutter arrived carrying three surveyors from New Zealand with three Manihiki natives that they had brought along as helpers. Johnny recalled that the New Zealand men were actually Coastwatchers. These were typically volunteers made up of colonial government officials, shopkeepers, missionaries and planters who would watch for Japanese activities during World War II. Coastwatchers were also organized under military intelligence to conduct guerilla operations and rescue downed pilots or crews of lost ships. It was often a lonely and isolated experience that was fraught with danger as the Japanese made efforts to exterminate these kinds of spies. Despite the Coastwatchers good work, Frisbie probably wondered why they were on uninhabited Suwarrow Island and felt intruded. He selfishly thought, "What were these white men doing here, surveying *his* island?"

Incredibly, shortly after the arrival of the coast watchers, Frisbie spotted another cutter called the *Vagus* round the point at one of the islets. He described the boat, "The finest little vessel I've ever seen, heard of, or dreamed of." The *Vagus'* owner was John Pratt, an Englishman who had sailed the boat via the West Indies and Panama. Later at Palmerston Island, Pratt was joined by Ronald Powell, who helped navigate the cutter to the islands of the northern Cooks and was also an old friend of Frisbie. Suwarrow Island's population grew to the unlucky number of thirteen and the group got along splendidly. But little would they know that within a few days after the *Vagus'* arrival, the island would be hit by one of the fiercest hurricanes in the region that a human being would ever experience.

The hurricane that devastated the island of Suwarrow struck around February 19, 1942. The sea crashed again and again across the island with incredible speed carrying before it smaller trees and huge masses of coral torn from the reef. Nineteen out of every twenty coconut trees were destroyed and the boats that the visitors arrived in were lost. The clothes were torn from everyone's bodies. Miraculously, all thirteen people survived. They had lashed themselves to the five remaining giant *tamanu* trees and rode out the storm; it was all they could do. Frisbie believed that because these giant trees were so close together their roots interlocked solidifying an unbreakable grip within the ground. By the end of the storm only six out of the twenty-five islets would remain and half of their land areas were gone.

Everything that Frisbie and his cowboys owned was lost including most of his correspondences and manuscripts. Fortunately, his typewriter was saved because it was in the tree house during the storm. Losing his manuscripts seemed like a burden was lifted. Frisbie wrote to Hall after the storm regarding his manuscripts and said, "I am glad that my old manuscripts are lost. There must have been a million words of them, monstrous children begotten often enough when I had mistaken the heat of madness for flashes of genius."

Surviving the hurricane was the stuff of legends. Whenever the Frisbie name was mentioned, one cannot help think of him and his children lashed to the trees for survival. It was just something that not many people have done in their lives. I refrain from writing about the hurricane in detail as so much has already been written about the Frisbie's harrowing ordeal. In 1943 the *Atlantic Monthly* published a series of Frisbie's articles titled, "The Story of an Island." These articles were about his time of living on Suwarrow Island and surviving the hurricane. This marvelous depiction would end up in his book, *The Island of Desire* and was published a year later. Johnny would tell her version of enduring the hurricane in both of her books.

Five weeks after the hurricane the same boat that brought the Frisbies to Suwarrow, *Taipi*, called on the island. The captain told Frisbie that when he first saw what was left of Suwarrow he thought he would have nothing to do ashore but to search the rubble for dead bodies. The captain was dumbstruck when Frisbie told him that he and his cowboys wish to remain on the atoll despite enduring such problems as mosquitoes, flies, land crabs and sunburn. If anyone could live off the land, it was the Frisbies. The *Taipi* weighed anchor and sailed off leaving some rations behind for the family. It was unsure if this was when the other survivors finally got a chance to leave the island. The schooner's captain, Andy Thompson, wrote to Hall and gave him an update on Frisbie and said that the schooner, *Tagua*, went to their relief. He also said that he had sent the family some canned milk, onions, potatoes, rice and other edible items. Perhaps the *Taipi* was confused with the *Tagua*, or perhaps, two boats called in at Suwarrow. Nevertheless, Frisbie chose to remain on this devastated island. He would call it his "Adventure in Solitude." Johnny would later recall that it was the *Tagua* that would take her family to Manihiki atoll.

CHAPTER SIX

SOUTH OF THE EMPTY SPACE

Manihiki Island is a triangular coral atoll that is about 290 miles east of Pukapuka. The atoll is a continuous rim of reef comprising of forty tiny islets that encircle a two and half miles wide lagoon. Black pearls could be found in this body of water, which was the island's greatest asset. One of the first navigators of the Pacific, Pedro Fernandes de Queiros, gave the island the name, "*Gente Hermosa*," which means, "Beautiful People," in the early 1600s. Trader Tom Richards described Manihiki from the deck of a ship as "a jewel set in a silver sea." Johnny quoted her father's dreamlike recollection of Manihiki when he visited the island before he was married. She wrote, "I think this is the most beautiful island of them all. And the women here are as lovely as their island. They are so beautiful that in the past one of their greatest dangers was being kidnapped by sailors. Wait until you see them. I think that I shall look around for a wife here." Fanny Stevenson and her husband, Louis, mentioned how beautiful the people were on Manihiki during their cruise on the *Janet Nichol*. Fanny wrote, "It is significant that Manihiki is always conspicuously marked on even the smallest maps of the world, no doubt from the fact that its delightful people have attracted so much attention from seamen that the place has acquired an artificial importance out of all proportion to its few square miles of reef."

Although Frisbie and his cowboys arrived on Manihiki in tattered clothes, they were in good spirits and happy to be back on the island. Frisbie had fond memories of Manihiki from the time he spent there when traveling throughout the Pacific on the *Motuovini*. They settled in the house of an old friend who was also the Resident Agent of the island on Tapuaikaha Islet. This lonely islet was about five acres wide and three miles from the main village of Tauhunu. The only neighbors were seafowl and land crabs that crawled about in the bush.

During their stay in Manihiki, Frisbie confided with Hall by telling him in a letter that he was not working, had not written anything for six months and felt not the slightest desire to ever work again. "I am at peace with the world and with myself, and am quite content to catch a fish, read a book, smoke my pipe, and teach my children the three "R's." The only trouble that weighed on his conscience was that of his children. Johnny vexed him most of all. He said that he was so fond of his eldest daughter that it made him miserable. He knew that she should be attending school, but he did not have the means to send her. Frisbie doted over her and wrote, "She is much more of a European or an American than I am. She has naturally nice ways, fine perceptions and a sense of integrity." He loved his other children too, but he believed that they acted more like "savages."

After the death of his wife, the islanders on Pukapuka expected Frisbie to take a new wife, but he defiantly resisted the easy temptations of other maidens. He was more interested in proving to everyone that he could raise his children alone. The beautiful women on Manihiki, however, would prove to be difficult for Frisbie to ignore. He fell in love with an enchanting twenty-year old native at first sight named, Esetera. She was mature, graceful and a perfect hedonist who won the affections of Frisbie's children. Johnny mentioned that Esetera had a sweet face and a kind heart. Her philosophy was like that of most other Pacific Islanders: eat, sleep and enjoy life. Frisbie did not waste any time wooing her and she did not waste any time being wooed. They married each other in a simple ceremony that took place at the administration building in the largest Manihikian village of Tauhunu. Esetera's family were very happy for her because she was marrying a white man and presented the new couple with many mats, live pigs and baskets of baked chicken and pork. For the rest of 1942 Frisbie, his new bride, and the cowboys lived in harmony on the islet of Tapuaeka.

It is difficult for a writer at any level to stay away from his next story for a long period of time. Even Frisbie who desired to give up his calling could not help but to sit at his typewriter. His creative juices were flowing once again. As Esetera played and fished with the cowboys, Frisbie started clanking away on the keys. It was a peaceful time living on Manihiki. But the threat of war was spreading throughout the Pacific Islands and the Japanese army was invading island after island. It would be Frisbie's countrymen who were forced into stopping them. The call to support the American war cause was too great for Frisbie to ignore and so he began to plan how he could best be useful.

In early 1943 Frisbie and his family sailed with Andy Thompson on the *Tiare Taporo* to Rarotonga. As they made their approach, Johnny described her first visit to the "down south" island and wrote, "The mountains are pointed high, with sheer exposed cliffs like naked arms reaching for the sky. The puffy clouds sit on the tips of them as if playing some gigantic game, like king-of-the-mountain, until they are edged off or joined by others."

I can recall back in 2002 while volunteering on Rarotonga; I took an outing on a boat mostly to get a view of the island from the sea. After a few miles out to sea, I got seasick and spent most of the trip below decks. On the way back to shore I was determined to take in the view of the island and mustered enough energy to crawl back on deck. By this time of the trip a storm hit the boat that didn't help my seasickness. On deck I gazed upon the jagged edges of the interior of the island through the mist. Like Johnny's description of the first time she saw Rarotonga, the clouds were swallowing the mountains whole. The island was eerie yet intriguing, especially on this windswept afternoon. I imagined myself as one of the crew on Cook's *Endeavor* or Bligh's *Bounty*, gazing inquisitively for the first time upon an island that potentially played to your dreams and desires. Then I vomited and in an instant my daydream was broken. I was green as the water that day and embarrassingly felt like a landlubber. I quickly looked around the boat to see if anyone saw me hurling my lunch into the sea. Fortunately, most of my shipmates were below decks staying out of the wind and the rain and were seasick themselves. I tried to make my way back below and felt like a crab fighting against a strong current. But I made it. Once below I prayed for a speedy return to the dock, and as I looked at the faces of other seasick colleagues, I knew that I wasn't alone in this prayer.

As the *Tiare Taporo* approached the Avarua jetty, Frisbie noticed his son, Charles, in the small crowd that had gathered to greet the boat. Charles was thirteen years old and Frisbie could not hide his excitement on seeing him and jumped off the boat before its lines were even secured. Johnny noted that her father was so elated to see his son that he grabbed Charles and lifted him high in the air and then shook his hand, kissed him and shook his hand once again. As he introduced Charles to his siblings, grandaunt Piki-Piki was close by and was not too thrilled about the reunion. She was afraid that this meeting would enhance the possibility of losing her adopted son. When the time came for Frisbie and his children to return to Pukapuka, he wanted to take Charles with them. A big fight ensued between him and Piki-Piki over whether or not the boy should be allowed to come with the rest of the family. In the end the desperate, stolid aunt won the battle and Charles remained in Rarotonga with her; she would never let him out of her sight again.

The Frisbies lived in a house outside the main town of Avarua and tried to settle in with their new surroundings. The cowboys began a formal education at a school in town for the first time in their lives while Frisbie applied for a job with the U.S. Navy Intelligence Department in hopes of helping his country during this time of war. The family was living from hand to mouth in Rarotonga and some of the bills that were piling up truly concerned Frisbie. When Hall's family traveled to the United States to visit relatives and left him behind, he wrote to Frisbie about the loneliness that he was experiencing. Frisbie returned a response by stating that every time that he was away from his family he wallowed in the depth of depression. He said, "But, Hall, what fools we are! In reality we are suffering from an unacknowledged form of egotism." Frisbie anticipated the misery of separation from his kids should he be given the job with the U.S. Navy Intelligence Service. At this time, however, it was a moot point since Frisbie had not received a reply from the agency.

Frisbie fancied himself doing great things for the American war cause. He tried several times to become involved with the U.S. armed forces and to volunteer his time doing whatever job that he hoped could make a difference. As nothing truly came to fruition, Frisbie grew invariably frustrated. He did take the opportunity to write about his observation on the relationship of American servicemen and the islanders. He wrote an article for the *Pacific Islands Monthly* titled, "Economic Debauchery of Polynesians by Friendly Troops," that was published in January 1944. It was an objective look on how the American troops affected the cultural and economic life of the South Pacific people. He believed that the islanders' material welfare improved according to the standards of western civilization but at the cost of losing their culture. Because of this, they refused to work their plantations, go fishing, and make handicrafts. Frisbie feared that when the American troops withdrew from the island the natives would despise going back to their old way of life. He was right as it took decades for some islanders to return to their heritage, while others never did and still have not to this day.

Esetera was having the time of her life on Rarotonga. The

town was bigger than any place she was used to while living on Manihiki. It was full of activities and intriguing people. She enjoyed the picture shows and partying at night with the Rarotongan women who she found made friends easily. Many of the island women believed that she was too young to have married a forty-seven-year-old man and predicted that trouble lay ahead. Johnny noticed that civilization had been too much for her stepmother. The sweet and gentle young lady from Manihiki turned into a philanderer, drunkard and a "good-for-nothing" woman. She would leave the house at night and not come back until morning. This would be trouble in any household in any country.

Esetera's attitude towards the children had also changed. She became mean and nasty and would unnecessarily scold the cowboys for every little thing that they did wrong. During this time Frisbie was experiencing health problems and one day when he came home after spending a few weeks in the hospital, he found that no food was prepared for his children's lunch. It was an eye-opening moment for him. Johnny recalled the disappointing frown that formed on her father's face. When Esetera returned home, he confronted her about leaving the children alone. After a few days, her late-night dalliances got her in trouble once again and Frisbie realized that their marriage was not going to work and decided it would be best to send her back home despite her desperate supplications to remain on Rarotonga. A couple of weeks later an unhappy and sobbing Esetera was put on the *Tiare Taporo* that was heading back to Manihiki. The event depressed Frisbie and made him realize that he would never find a woman as good as his Pukapukan wife, Ngatokorua.

The Frisbies moved to a quaint house in Aorangi Village

where they would remain for the next year. It was doubtful that Frisbie's application for the U.S. Navy Intelligence Service was ever accepted. He was a single parent once again teaching his children manners and helping them with their schoolwork. Johnny recalls that at this time the household developed the "Slave-labor Gang" where each child was given a specific chore each day. Frisbie's health at this time was not at its best. Since he was living close to his good friend Andy Thompson, the two often got together to share stories. The two old friends had no trouble entertaining one another into the wee hours of the night.

About this time Frisbie's health started to deteriorate once again. George Weller, who was an American correspondent for the *Chicago Daily News*, was traveling through Rarotonga in 1943 and got to be acquainted with Frisbie. Weller also knew Hall in Tahiti and told him about Frisbie's frail health. He reported to Hall an account of Frisbie's relationship towards his children. Weller said that it was Johnny, although only ten, who was the responsible head of the family and looked after her younger siblings far better than her father was able to do.

DoubleDay, Doran & Co. published Frisbie's fourth book, *The Island of Desire: The Story of a South Sea Trader*, in 1944. The format and theme of the book was very similar to that of his first three books. It was a collection of short stories that were originally published by the *Atlantic Monthly*. The stories were an engaging, autobiographical account of his marriage to Desire (Ngatokorua), his four children, the death of Desire and the "Robinson Crusoe" existence that he and his children experienced. It included trading activities, the gossip and local affairs on Pukapuka and the devastating hurricane that caught him and his family by surprise on Suwarrow Island. *The Island of Desire* certainly delivered an authentic feel for the South Pacific and was full of romance and adventure. Still, Frisbie did not feel that it was his "*Moby Dick.*"

By the end of 1944 Frisbie grew tired of Rarotonga and wanted to return to Pukapuka. They got passage on the Tiare Taporo, but to pay half of their ticket, Frisbie was hired as the chief engineer aboard the ship. During the journey their first port-of-call was Manihiki where almost immediately the children came across Esetera sitting on the front porch of her house singing to her baby. According to Johnny she had married a Manihikian Islander and appeared to be very happy. Esetera did not seem to harbor any hard feelings towards the cowboys or her ex-husband and invited them to a Manihikian dinner with the hope of seeing Frisbie again. Purposely, perhaps, Frisbie did not attend the feast because he was away with Captain Thompson sharing bush beer. Esetera in true island fashion was not going to let the children leave without food, thus she packed a basket full of baked chicken, drinking nuts and dried pauas (mantrap clams) before sending them on their way back to their father. In response Frisbie kindly sent her a treasure box consisting of combs, soap, hair oil and a cashmere bouquet powder.

It was not too long before the Frisbies returned to the boat, and after four days at sea, they sighted Penrhyn Island named in honor of its discovery by Captain William Crofton Sever of H.M.S. *Lady Penrhyn*, who landed on August 8, 1788. The natives called the island "Tongareva" which meant, "south of the empty space." Penrhyn is the most far-flung island of the Cook Islands and is about 200 miles to the northeast of Manihiki. It is one of the largest atolls in the

Pacific Islands. Frisbie met many American army officers who arrived on the island in 1942, built a runway as an alternate supply route from Hawaii through Australia and New Zealand, and stayed for four years. The American GIs seemed to have an endless supply of whiskey and cigarettes. Frisbie was at ease with these officers and after a night of reverie decided to remain on Penrhyn. He told Captain Thompson, "Yes, Captain, I decided to stay here with my family. These army officers need a sane American around." Then he yelled to his kids, "Children! Cowboys! Get our things. We're staying!"

For much of their time on the island they lived with Philip Wooton in Omoka, the biggest and most modern village on the island. The cowboys loved it. They enjoyed mingling with the American soldiers. They watched American movies, ate chocolate bars and even tried smoking cigarettes. Frisbie thought the soldiers were being a bad influence on his children and thus moved the family about three miles across the lagoon to Moto Toto. The cowboys were unhappy about the move at first, but quickly got used to their new environment. It was not long before they started having adventures in the unusual reef. Sadly, their enjoyment would not last long as Frisbie became very ill once again and began hemorrhaging.

By doctors' orders at the American army dispensary, it was decided that Frisbie should to be sent to a hospital in Pago-Pago, American Samoa, if he had any chance of getting better. Frisbie's departure was rough on him and his children, but everyone believed that if he was going to get better, he had to go to Pago-Pago. The cowboys would remain on Penrhyn living in one of Wooton's empty houses. They were practically unsupervised, but Johnny remembered that they cooked, washed and usually went to bed at the right hour.

On the plane to American Samoa, Frisbie's reputation as a South Seas writer and maverick had preceded him, when he met a young American lieutenant by the name of James A. Michener who was quite fascinated by the newly acquired evacuee. Michener described Frisbie as a tuberculosis patient with deep eyes and a protruding lower jaw. He said of Frisbie, "He looked like the dying Robert Louis Stevenson." During the flight the two hit it off tremendously talking about the Pacific and writing, which allowed a friendship to ensue.

Michener would eventually go on to have a very lucrative writing career and add his name to the list of South Seas writers. In his early writing days he penned a couple of books of short stories that would become classics. These included the Pulitzer Prize winner, *Tales of the South Pacific*, published in 1947, and *Return to Paradise* that was published four years later. The latter contained a story that was modeled after the Frisbie's trader life. Later, Michener would capture the essence of Frisbie when he stated, "I liked Frisbie. I respected his basic honesty. If ever I knew a man who destroyed himself through the search for beauty, Frisbie was that man."

Frisbie found his time in the Pago-Pago hospital frustrating, maddening and scary. In November of 1945 he wrote to Hall describing his ordeal, first stating that he had off and on been in a hospital since the first of April and that he had been close to death on three occasions. "They have given me seven blood transfusions, and I have lost count of the plasma and dextrose," he told Hall. Frisbie's illness was never truly diagnosed. He would get better one day and then without warning he would become dizzy, faint and lose as much as a gallon of blood in one hemorrhage. As the radio in the hospital blared until ten at night, he dreamed of returning to the peace and stillness of Pukapuka. Frisbie could not stand the programs that were coming over the radio and sarcastically blamed them for his hemorrhages. He complained to Hall, "Why should one worry about atom bombs destroying civilization when civilization produces the kind of art heard over the radio, and the kind of humor that Jack Benny vomits out to the public? Oh, Hall, I gotta get out of here!"

Miraculously Frisbie's health was well enough that he could leave the hospital. He took a job as the acting principal at a local high school for boys and immediately sent for his children. They got to ride in a plane for the first time in their lives; it was a terrific adventure for them. No doubt, however, that the fate of Frisbie's children if he should die was the impetus of him gaining his health. He confided to Hall about this issue once again and wrote, "It is appalling to think of my beloved Johnny becoming a little whore on the streets of Pago. They don't make daughters any finer than Florence Ngatokorua (Johnny) Frisbie." When his children arrived at the airport, he forgot about his worries and screamed, "There they are! My cowboys!" The reunion was joyful. They had so much to talk about. Frisbie shared the good news that he had finished his latest novel, *Amaru*, and that Doubleday & Company would publish it.

Amaru was Frisbie's first true fictionalized novel. It tells the adventures of a young American man in search of fortune in pearls on a distant islet. Most of the reviews of the novel were lukewarm. A reviewer from the *New York Times,* however, was more favorable when he wrote, "The reader could hardly find a more pleasant escape than the pages of *Amaru* provide. Any resemblance between the Pacific islands in this book and those which are at present subject to examination and attack by our armed forces is strictly coincidental." When the novel was published, the war was in its last year. Frisbie chose to write about the South Seas because he knew it in its pure, unmolested self and not about the horrors that the war produced in the region and known throughout the rest of the world. Personally, I thought the book was terrific and was by far my favorite Frisbie piece of work. It had it all: adventure, passion, an unpredictable villain, a ghost island, shark attacks and a buried treasure of pearls. What more could you want? It was set against the unmistaken romance of South Seas islands where the reader can smell the salt air, feel the balmy, romantic nights and see the changing azures of the sea. Additionally, there was a back-story that tied in nicely with that of the story about the main character.

After a few months living with his children on Pago Pago, Frisbie decided to move to Western Samoa on the main island of Upolu that was about seventy-five miles to the northeast. He cited that one of the reasons for this move was because he got to know too many American Navy men who enjoyed taking him to local bars. Alcohol not only distracted him from writing and spending time with his children, it was detrimental to his health especially during this time of his life. On the first of January 1946 the Frisbie clan sailed to Apia. Almost immediately Frisbie became instant friends with a German by the name of R. Berking. Frisbie's new friend invited him and his cowboys to live with him on his ranch near the village of Letogo in the central north coast of Upolu. Johnny recalls that Berking was a large red-faced man who was attracted to the backside of women and was married to a portly Samoan girl. "The fatter the better," he said. Although he and Frisbie had little in common and seemed to disagree on just about every subject, they did enjoy each other's company. A friendship grew like two white men in the South Seas who were isolated from their native lands.

Western Samoa was also the place where Robert Louis Stevenson lived from 1889 until his death in 1894. Although Stevenson was one of Frisbie's inspirational writers, the two men lived completely different lives in Samoa despite that both suffered from ill health. Stevenson and his wife, Fanny, bought 314 acres of land in Vailima that was not too far from the main town of Apia. At the base of Mount Vaea the couple built a mansion that had five bedrooms, a library and a large ballroom that would accommodate a hundred dancers. While Frisbie often lived from hand to mouth, the Stevensons lived in style backed by many publishing successes such as *Treasure Island, Kidnapped* and *The Strange Case of Dr. Jekyll and Mr. Hyde*. Oysters were shipped on ice from New Zealand, Bordeaux wine was brought by the cask from France and bottled at Vailima and an 1840 vintage Madeira was poured on special occasions. Every evening they dressed formally for dinner with the exception of wearing shoes and were served by Samoans who wore tartan lava-lavas in honor of Stevenson's Scottish heritage. The Stevenson's lavish lifestyle baffled the Samoans as they could not understand how a man could make money by writing. They believed that Stevenson was a man that had much mana (spiritual strength) and used to love sitting with him listening to stories especially ones about Samoan culture, language and politics. When Stevenson died, the Samoans cleared a path to the top of Mount Vaea, and there the author was buried.

In 2011, I happened to visit Apia for a regional archives conference. As a fan of Stevenson's work, particularly his

South Seas stories, I made sure to take some time from the conference and visit his estate. After Stevenson's death, Samoa's head of state lived in Stevenson's house at Vailima until cyclones in the early 1990s severely damaged the house. Today it is a museum.

Robert L. Stevenson's House, Vailima, Samoa

As one enters the front parlor room, the first thing that catches everyone's eye is the fireplace. It's an odd sight to see a fireplace in an environment that never seems to drop below 75°F (24°C). It was one of those items that reminded Stevenson of his beloved Scotland. I wondered how often he actually used it. The Samoans certainly would have put it to use for cooking food. The mansion was just big enough to get yourself lost for a spell, which on a Thursday afternoon was absolutely fine. I practically had the house to myself to peruse the 19th century furniture and the Samoan knick-knacks on the walls. This was a dream come true. I then took a seat at his desk. An employee walked by and didn't seem to care too much as to what I was doing. "*Talofa*," (the Samoan word for "hello") I said to the man. "Can you take my picture?" He took my camera. I sat up straight, and "click." Then I wondered, *I don't think that was an employee who took my picture*. It was just another guest visiting the museum. Stevenson also had a small writing table attached to his bed that he would use on those days when his health was bad. I wanted to try it out badly, but thought better of it. I continued on my self-made tour of the house.

Conquering Mount Vaea and visiting Stevenson's grave was also on my itinerary for the day. I have read that the views overlooking his estate and Vailima were spectacular. I overzealously started my assent up the 472-meter-high mountain and quickly realized that the path that was carved over a hundred years ago was difficult to navigate. Apparently, there were two paths that would lead you to the top, and one was more strenuous than the other. I had no idea which one I was on, but it wasn't easy. Half way up a group of Samoans caught up to me. A round of *"Talofas"* sung out as they passed me. I tried to keep up but they were like mountain goats wearing flip-flops. I didn't have to wonder about who was more fit. Finally, I reached the top out of breath and thought to myself, *Damn it, Stevenson, you're going to make me join you*. Stevenson's grave was quite impressive. I instantly understood how it could be a place of pilgrimage for fans of his. Even the non-fan would find the place very tranquil, moving and a source of inspiration. The trek back down was even more treacherous than the climb up, but I had an advantage I was wearing shoes. I easily caught up to my Samoan friends, and another round of *"Talofas"* was called out as I merrily passed them.

As his children entertained themselves on the ranch, Frisbie worked feverishly on two projects. He first edited Johnny's book about the adventurous travels of the Frisbie family titled, *Miss Ulysses from Puka-Puka*. The book was written when Johnny was between the ages of twelve and fourteen and in three languages that included English, Rarotongan and Pukapukan. Frisbie noted that when Johnny wrote exposition, description and imagery, she resorted to one of the Polynesian languages and that he had a hard time interpreting her mood, humor and ingenious philosophy of life. He praised the book in the introduction, "The finished work is, I believe, unique in South Sea literature, being the first book, to my knowledge, written by a native South Sea Islander. Johnny looks at civilization with eyes both appreciative and amused, incredulous and, at times, disapproving."

Frisbie's statement regarding Johnny being the first native South Sea Islander writer should not go unnoticed. It begs the question: why did written literature by the indigenous population take so long to emerge? Some theories to explain the slow development of writers in the region point to obvious reasons, including the fact that the islands had a very strong oral tradition and that it took time for the islanders to become confident in English and its use as a language of creative expression. Other factors for the slow growth of Pacific Island writers could be attributed to limited resources, a reliance on colonial government officials and employees for cultural documentation, and the lack of universities or access to higher learning. The indifference of missionaries and high-ranking administrators towards indigenous literature also played a major role in the lethargic movement of writers.

MR. MOONLIGHT OF THE SOUTH SEAS

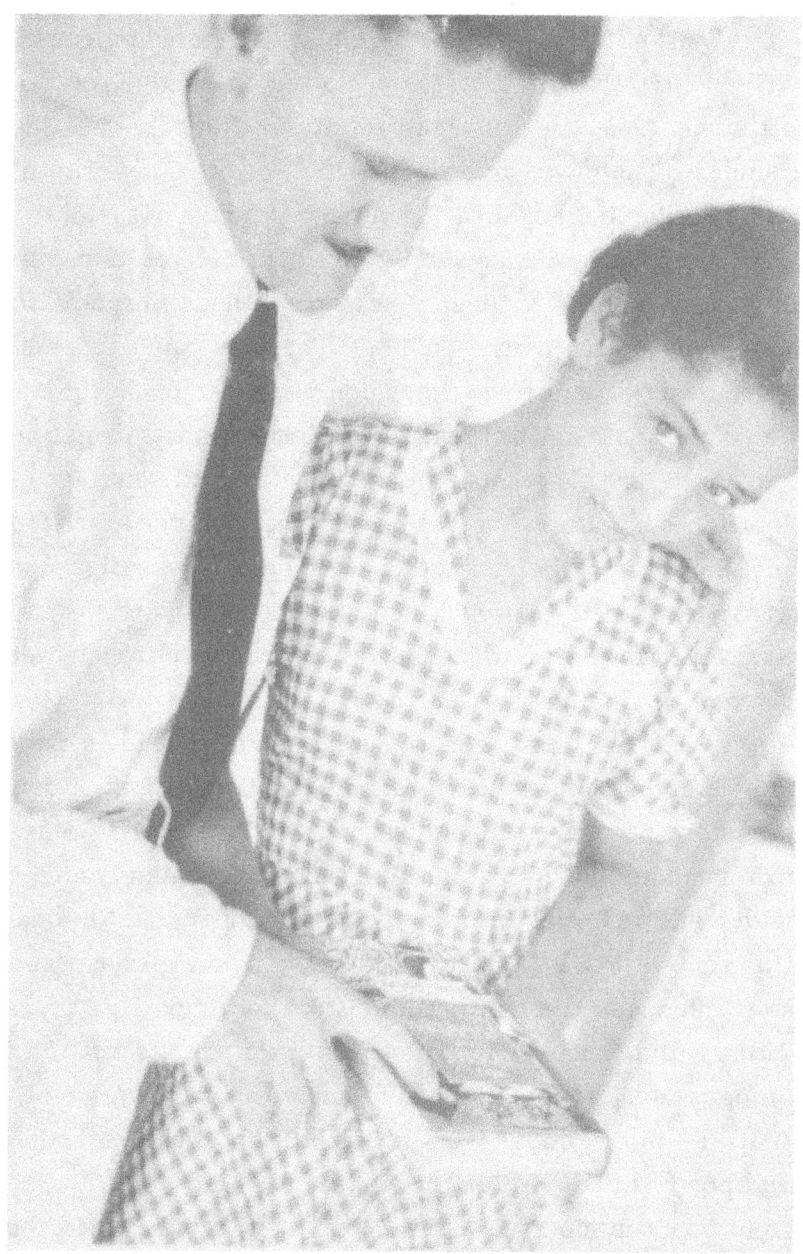

Frisbie with Johnny and Her New Book

It was not until the 1960s when the development of written literature in the region started to change for the better. In 1965, the University of Papua New Guinea was established, followed by the formation of the University of South Pacific (USP) in Suva, Fiji in 1967. Although both universities produced students who wrote creative pieces mainly in English, the USP's student newspaper called Unispac also started to attract writers in 1968. The newspaper inspired other creative islanders in the region, which led to the formation of the South Pacific Creative Arts Society and its magazine Mana in 1973. This became the impetus for a different type of South Seas literature that was very distinct from the American and European writers of the past. These new indigenous writers examined their own identity and explored real island issues and concerns of the people in far more depth than ever before.

Two of the more modern and influential leaders with unique indigenous voices were Epeli Hau'ofa and Albert Wendt, respectively. Hau'ofa was born in Papua New Guinea to Tongan missionary parents and eventually would graduate with a PhD in Social Anthropology at the Australian National University. He was a poet, professor, scholar, essayist, and storyteller. He authored the short-story collection *Tales of the Tikongs* (published in 1994) and *Kisses in the Nederends*, an unforgettable satire, published one year later. Arguably, Hau'ofa's most famous work is a collection of essays, fiction and poetry titled, *We Are the Ocean*, published in 2008. The collection contains the essay *Our Sea of Islands*, where he disagrees with the idea that Pacific Islanders were separated by the sea, and argues instead that they are actually connected by the ocean. In 1997 Hau'ofa established the

Oceania Center of Arts, Culture and Pacific Studies at USP's Laucala Campus in Suva, Fiji where he remained as its director until his death in 2009.

Albert Wendt was a Samoan novelist and poet who endeavored to contradict the romanticized South Sea stories popularized by American and European writers. His fiction often showed the traditions and attitudes of the *papalagi* (people descended from Europeans) and depicted their effect on Samoan culture. A couple of his earlier novels include the Polynesian version of King Lear titled *Pouliulu*, published in 1977, and the Samoan family saga, *Leaves of the Banyan*, printed in 1979. As Wendt's writing style evolved, his unique voice blended Polynesian history, myth and oral traditions with contemporary issues. His 2009 mythological epic of *The Adventures of Vela* won the 2010 Commonwealth Writers' Prize for best book in the Southeast Asia and South Pacific category. In 2012 Wendt was a recipient of the prestigious Prime Minister's Award for Literary Achievement for Fiction, New Zealand's highest literary award.

Frisbie was proud of his daughter's proclivity toward creative writing. He wrote to Hall stating that Johnny had made the grade where he failed as a writer. Recognition of this fact had given him a new lease on life. He felt that she would go far because she started a career in writing so early. Frisbie, perhaps, was consoled by the thought that if anything should happen to him, Johnny would be able to take care of her siblings through her writing. He mentioned how wonderful it was planning work with Johnny. "She takes such keen interest in it and has so many good ideas of her own."

The second book that Frisbie was incessantly working on during this time was his own latest endeavor, *Dawn Sails*

North, which would be his last novel. This was the one that he hoped would be his masterpiece, his *Moby Dick*. He worked day and night on the story and this worried his children. They feared that too much work would make their father sick again. Johnny recalled that he was experimenting with new sentence structures and new words. When he slept, he dreamed of new ideas to add to his novel and would awake in the middle of the night to write them down. Frisbie's mood changed while working on the book. When visitors came to the ranch, he had little time to chat with them, which was very unlike him. Perhaps, his behavioral changes were caused from not feeling well. His right leg swelled again, and along with it, a fever set in. This was another cause of worry for the cowboys who would see their father lay motionless in his bed as if he were dead. When good health returned, he would work on the projects until he collapsed with exhaustion. In March he wrote to Hall that he was about halfway done with *Dawn Sails North* and he hoped he could finish it by the end of the year. He also shared that even with his hours curtailed, he could do more and better work than formerly.

In another letter to Hall, the optimistic Frisbie was dreaming of the future that he believed was the children's future. "I have the sweetest little family on the face of the earth, and in it, one true genius (referring to Johnny) of a high order," Frisbie proudly wrote. He shared that his children went to Leifiifi, which was the best South Seas school. He also wrote that they were the best dressed, had the best manners and everyone was delighted with them. "My only cause for worry is the old one, money. I am worth just twenty pounds as this writing, and I owe three hundred, and so, financially, I stand at minus 280 pounds. But I'm alive and I look forward to Johnny's future." The two continued to work on *Miss Ulysses* together. They were nearing the finish, but were having trouble developing an ending. He told Hall, "Maybe something will work out, like my conveniently dying to bring it to a proper climax." The book would be published that same year and would eventually be awarded a second edition by the Dockside Sailing Press in 2016.

Frisbie felt that he had never fully recovered from all of his hemorrhages and his ailing days at the hospital in Pago Pago. He told Hall that he was a sick man and that he hoped to last two or three more years for the sake of his children, but he was not optimistic about this. About this time Hall received a photograph of Frisbie and his children and noticed that his old friend still had thick and dark hair. He found that Frisbie's face was that of a youthful old man but haggard and drawn with an expression upon it of deep suffering. Frisbie thought that he could turn himself over to Navy doctors in Pago Pago, and since he was a World War I veteran, they would be obliged to send him back to the United States. "But where could I leave the children? There is no one this side of Puka-Puka who could or would take care of them should I leave, or die. This is why I want to return soon to Rarotonga." Frisbie believed that from Rarotonga his children could at least be able to return to his wife's relatives on Pukapuka. He thought that although they may lose what he taught them in terms of schooling, at least they would be able to live a healthy life as savages. "Who knows? The Puka Puka kind of savagery might be better for them than the "civilized" savagery prevailing in the world today."

A lifetime seemed to have passed since the last time Frisbie and Hall saw one another. They had both married, had children, went on adventures and made a career in writing albeit with various degrees of success. They tried to get together on a few occasions, but it was just never meant to be, as they seemed to miss each other each time. Fortunately, the two friends did keep a relationship by corresponding throughout the years. In early 1947 Frisbie was yearning to see Hall, perhaps, one last time. It was his ill health that made him long for the old days when he used to sit on Hall's verandah and discuss life, boats and literature. One day at the ranch Johnny remembers her father entering a room and enthusiastically exclaimed, "Johnny, Jakey, Elaine, Nga! Sit on the floor and listen to me. We have just enough money to fly by plane to Tahiti and visit Hall whom I have not seen in over ten years. I've got to see him about a new book. Are you ready to travel again?"

"When?" the children screamed.

"Within the week," he answered.

The family arrived in Papeete and were eager to meet with Hall only to receive the unfortunate news that Frisbie's old friend had been away in California to attend his daughter's wedding. It was a crushing blow to Frisbie. Distraught, he would spend hours sitting on the parapet outside of Hall's house. He wanted desperately to rush inside but he knew that Hall was not there to welcome him. Frisbie left a letter for Hall to read when he returned from California. The defeated, somber tone of the letter described his walk along the waterfront and seeing the copra schooners and Low Island cutters moored along the seawall that used to excite him. Now they no longer interested him. He would finish his letter by admitting that he hated to leave such a sour note, but it was the only way to let Hall know that he was there.

The letter also showed how much Tahiti had changed since Frisbie first came to the island. He stated that Tahiti was like a "Lost Island" (a reference to one of Hall's novels). "Of course, there were the same glorious mountains," he lamented. "More than likely they look no different now than they did when Polynesians first saw them a thousand years ago. They are not even conscious of the human insects living on the fringe of lowland around the coast." He went on to say how he did not meet any new "insects" and that Papeete was crawling with so many French people that he termed, "*fonctionnaire*" insects. "I don't wonder that they want to get away from France, but it's hard on the Tahitians having so many." By this time the town of Papeete grew as the main economic, administrative and religious center for the region. The region was established as French Polynesia and was comprised of five groups of islands that are now known as the Society Islands, the Tuamotu Archipelago, the Gambier Islands, the Marquesas Islands and the Austral Islands.

The relationship between the Polynesians and the French became somewhat strained beginning in the last half of the 20th century. During World War II the island of Bora Bora, in the Society Islands, became a refueling station for United States forces. American influence helped inspire French Polynesian nationalism among Tahiti residents and the desire for more cultural, economic and political freedom. In 1946 the colony became an overseas territory of France and a territorial assembly was created to manage local affairs. In the late 1940s an independence movement emerged in the region that was led by a carpenter and war veteran named Pouvanaa Oopa. Oopa's pro-autonomy party gained the majority of seats in the territorial assembly in 1953 and 1957. In a referendum held in 1958, island voters chose to remain a territory of France rather than become independent and lose French economic aid. Today French Polynesia has greater autonomy than many other French territories. Despite the country's growing independence, there is still a need for greater attention to Polynesian culture that the indigenous people feel has been misrepresented and reduced to a sort of folklore by the romantic image that Europeans adopted.

Frisbie made the most of his stay in Papeete for several months visiting with old friends such as Andy Thompson and other captains who had come south for the cyclone season. Thompson wrote to Hall describing how Frisbie would wander aimlessly along the streets of Papeete looking for a few old friends. Many of his old friends had passed away including Charles Nordhoff who was, perhaps, the most notable and most recent missing friend. Although most of Nordhoff's writing successes were co-authored with Hall, he did pen a few stories that would achieve publication and a worldwide readership. These included *The Pearl Lagoon* published in 1924, *The Derelict* in 1928 and *In Yankee Windjammers* that made print in 1940. Nordhoff's marriage began to fall apart in Tahiti and he divorced his Tahitian wife in 1936. He moved back to California a few years later where he married Laura Grainger Whiley in 1941. Nordhoff died of an apparent heart attack on April 10, 1947, at age 60, at his home in Montecito. Some sources later indicated that he was depressed, drank heavily and committed suicide.

Frisbie's ill health forced him back in a hospital where he would remain for a couple of weeks. He did not approve of the way the doctors were treating him there, especially regarding the pains in his stomach. Because of this distrust in the medical options in Papeete, he was determined to go back to Rarotonga. When he found out that Thompson would be sailing the *Tiare Taporo* to Rarotonga, he made arrangements for his cowboys and himself to be on the boat. As the boat was leaving the port of Papeete, Frisbie spoke softly and dispiritedly to his children and said, "There is Papeete. The only value that place has for me now is the memories of days past, which I'll never see again." He then withdrew himself below decks before the island fell under the horizon.

For over two and half years Frisbie worked on *Dawn Sails North*. Distractions and health issues would bring the project to a crawl. At one point the editor wanted Frisbie to cut 10,000 words to get it down to 125,000 words "That seems to be our limit these days for a three-dollar novel." Discouraged, Frisbie did what they asked and resubmitted it. The editor wrote back and said, "I'm sorry that I had put you to so much work on *Dawn*, but I think you made a swell book of it and in the long run you will be glad you made the revisions. It reads so much better now." I on the other hand would have to disagree somewhat. Once I found a copy of the out-of-print book, I was extremely excited as if I had dug-up lost treasure. Although I enjoyed the story, I did not find it to be a South Seas masterpiece. I labored through the book and settled on the fact that it was not as fun and intriguing as *Amaru*. I also had the feeling that it was missing chapters and wondered how the novel would have been if Frisbie did not have to cut as much as he did. The novel did capture the ambiance and the passion of the South Seas, and for that, the book has been given a prominent spot on my shelf.

Doubleday published *Dawn Sails North* posthumously in early 1949. It told the story of Sam Strickland who sailed out of

New Bedford for a South Seas island claimed by his grandfather. Once there he encountered a murder, lurid combats, a chase for pearls and eventually sailed north to San Francisco weathering heavy seas and short tempers from the crew. A *Herald-Tribune* reviewer wrote, "The author is at his best in his thrilling narrative of the voyage, and realism is strong enough to make one wonder why newspapers have not carried headlines of the island doings. Fascinating charts, island maps, and even house plans add to the story's interest." *The Saturday Review* also gave a positive review stating that the book was a stimulating, picturesque, and a virile voyage. "Mr. Frisbie, at the helm, steers an unswerving course." In a letter to Hall Frisbie felt that he produced a minor *Moby Dick*, "or, anyway, a book nearly as long," he quipped. He complained that Doubleday asked him to cut 250 pages and add more plot that he was compelled to do since they had advanced him some money. "So if you read *Dawn Sails North*, and I can't recommend it, bear in mind that it's not the book I wanted it to be."

Frisbie's health steadily declined during his stay in Rarotonga. As the kids grew older, he was unable to care for them properly and it was Johnny who took the motherly reins and supervised her siblings. A horse trainer by the name of Alf Rowan, who lived in Auckland, New Zealand, had proposed to Frisbie that he would take his sons and train them to be jockeys. Frisbie felt relieved that his sons would have a place where they would be safe and a chance to get involved in a profession. Charles went first and Jakey followed in October of 1948. When Jakey left, his sisters wept and Frisbie became very withdrawn and distant. Perhaps the thought that he would never see his boys again crept silently and painfully within his mind. He promised his girls that he would never part with one of his children ever again.

In late November 1948 Hall was in Papeete when a mutual friend of his and Frisbie's, who had recently arrived from Rarotonga, walked up to him and said, "Hall, I've bad news for you. Robert Frisbie is dead." Johnny recalls her father's last day on November 17 as a day when Frisbie was at home drinking with Thompson all day. After Thompson left, the girls put their father to bed. They washed his face, feet and arms and kissed him goodnight. Several hours later Johnny was awoken by moaning and went to her father. He managed to say, "Johnny don't ever leave me." She could tell that he was suffering from lockjaw. He groaned again and muttered, "Get the doctor." Johnny awoke her sister Elaine, and told her to watch their father while she fetched the doctor.

When she returned from the doctor's house, Frisbie said, "My little babies, I love you. Take good care of your sisters, Johnny." Johnny then remembers the panic that formed on his face and he desperately tried to get out of bed. His back muscles began to spasm forcing him to lie back down. The doctor finally arrived and gave Frisbie some shots and said an ambulance would come in the morning and take him to the hospital. The cowboys waited and waited for an ambulance but it never came. The absent ambulance forced Johnny to ride her bike to the hospital and seek help. Finally, one arrived in the late afternoon and took him to the hospital where he would later die. As Johnny took one last look at her father, she wondered what he had thought just before he drew his last breath. She hoped that her mother was there in spirit to help him along. No doubt that this would have been what Frisbie wanted most.

From Johnny's remembrance it was quite clear that Frisbie died from tetanus. This is a bacterial disease that causes muscle spasms and breathing problems. Signs or symptoms of the disease include lockjaw, or the inability to open the mouth, swallowing problems, painful convulsions and abnormal heart rhythms. It could lead to suffocation, respiratory failure and pneumonia. It was unclear as to how Frisbie contracted the disease, or if he was ever immunized. The most common way to get the disease is when the bacteria entered through an open wound, particularly a deep wound. The tetanus bacteria can live in the soil and be problematic in places such as the Pacific Islands. Many people living in the region during Frisbie's time carried on their business from day to day without wearing any kind of footwear and would have been at high-risk for contracting the disease. The tetanus vaccine was developed in the late 1920s and did not become available in the United States until the 1940s. It was rather conceivable that Frisbie was not immune to the disease, and with his already weakening and frail state of health, the tetanus bacteria brought death very quickly and painfully.

In *The Book of Puka-Puka* Frisbie recalled a day when William the Heathen and he were looking for a secluded area to share a bottle of rum that Captain Rasmussen had given them. They found an area in Pukapuka's largest graveyard near the Central Village council houses. Once settled, William began explaining to his friend how each headstone tells the story of the man buried beneath, even the ones that have no inscription chiseled on them. For example, a pointed headstone with a smaller painted one at the foot says that a great fisherman was buried there. Frisbie mused that an interesting book could be written about the gravestones of Pukapuka for they told many stories about those buried beneath and that each village had its own symbolism. It was not long before William jumped up and cried, "Carramba! I have decided on a fine stone for you, Ropati!" Frisbie raised his eyebrows to hear what his old friend had to say. "It will tell about your cowboy adventures, your two Puka-Puka wives, and everything else!"

Takitumu School, Rarotonga

Before I traveled back home at the end of my stint on Rarotonga in 2002, I made the final rounds on my bike to all my favorite haunts around the island. In the morning I made my way to the Takitumu School where a party was being given to my volunteer colleagues and myself for our help throughout the past few weeks. Headbands made of leis were placed on our heads and a Polynesian feast was laid out before us as if we were part of a royal family. Afterwards I made my way towards the town of Avarua to do some last-minute shopping and on the way I wanted to make sure that I stopped at two places. The first was at the Cook Islands Library and Museum where I said my fond farewell (no Isa Lei was sung) to the employees, volunteers and, of course, Johnny Frisbie. The second stop was at the Cook Islands Christian Church to seek out the gravesite of Robert Dean Frisbie. During my entire stay I didn't get a chance to visit the venerable church and felt that this would be my last chance.

The Cook Islands Christian Church was a white-washed coral building that was originally built in 1853. It didn't take me long to find Frisbie's grave in the small graveyard. Many of the above-ground graves, especially the older ones, were disfigured with a mold that turned the headstones black. Frisbie's headstone had also turned black, but I was still able to read the epitaph that simply displayed his name, rank in the U.S. military and the date of his birth and death. The word, "California" was printed under his name and was what caught my eye most of all. I looked around and at first thought what a lonely place for a man to be buried. It was a long way from California. I saw that the cemetery wasn't far from the ocean. Palm trees swayed in the light breeze as arrogant myna birds scurried along the ground like street punks looking for trouble. It was an idyllic, picture-perfect South Seas kind of day, and then I thought, "what an ideal and appropriate place for a man to be buried who dedicated his life to sharing the beauty of this very small and unique part of the world." Frisbie wasn't from Ohio, Texas or California. He was a Cook Islander and a Polynesian. He was adamant about the thought of not turning native while he lived in the region, but his ideas as well as his voice within his publications proudly couldn't have sounded more native. William the Heathen was right all those years ago: Frisbie's headstone told a wonderful, fascinating story.

Although the mutual friend of Hall and Frisbie's did not go into detail about the death of the author from Pukapuka, he did hand Hall a letter that was hastily written from another friend in Rarotonga. Hall took the letter to a little park on the waterfront to read it in private. This was the same park that he and Frisbie sat talking on the day of their first meeting nearly thirty years before. The letter confirmed that Frisbie had passed away. "It's a sad blow for all of us here and especially for the children," the letter read. "A Rarotonga woman has taken the children into her home at present. You will not be surprised to learn that Ropati died penniless and deeply in debt." Hall would later write his immediate action after he read the letter: "I looked towards the water and imagined a young healthy Frisbie unmoor a phantom boat, hoist sail, steer for the open sea, and giving me a farewell wave of the hand. I watched the little ghost-ship grow smaller and smaller heading west-by-north for the ghost of an island: Suwarrow, or Frisbie's island, as he loved to call it."

EPILOGUE
THE VOYAGE TO PO

James Normal Hall who was the first person that Robert Dean Frisbie met when he arrived in Tahiti in 1920 was quite the Renaissance man. He was an adventurer, soldier, airplane pilot, author, essayist and poet. Growing up in Colfax, Iowa, he was known as the "Woodshed Poet" for his love of literature and music and spending much of his childhood in his family's woodshed writing verse after verse. At age eleven he would write his most memorable poem within his woodshed. In fact, the first stanza would eventually become his epitaph:

> *Look to the Northward stranger*
> *Just over the hillside there*
> *Have you in your travels seen*
> *A land more passing fair.*

The second line would be changed slightly from, "*Just over the barn roof, there*" to "*Just over the hillside there*" to accommodate the vista of his gravesite that overlooked Matavai Bay

EPILOGUE

where many historic captains anchored their ships including, Bligh of the *Bounty*.

Hall enjoyed living in Tahiti and lived most of his last thirty years of life on the island where he made many excursions into the valleys and up the mountains. He would write that having been inland born he dreamed of islands. As most people rested during the midday siesta, Hall would wander the streets of Papeete and enjoyed having them all to himself. He recalls, "I love the hour between twelve and one when this island world falls under the enchantment of silence and sleep; but having been born in the higher latitudes, I can't accustom myself to the siesta. Sleep fails to come to me, and so, often, I set out for a stroll through the deserted streets." He would go on to poetically describe the sights, smells and sounds of the town befitting a South Seas writer. Hall adds:

> And, with my eyes, I hear the unfamiliar music of color that comes from gardens on either hand: the chiming of innumerable hibiscus bells; the clamorous trumpet-tones of the bougainvillea; flamboyant trees yearning like saxophones; and modest blossoms, deeply embowered in greenish gloom, giving forth arpeggios of cool notes like the tinkling of mandolins or the plucked strings of violin.

His solitary excursions would not last long as he made many friends on the island who loved spending time with him. He eventually settled in Arue and married Sarah Winchester. The couple would have two children together.

For the last two decades of his life, Hall was one of the best-known and successful writers in the English-speaking world. Several of his collaborative novels with Charles Nordhoff would not only sell well, but they were made into popular movies from the 1930s to the 1950s. It was said that a more distinctive voice and an engaging personality would emerge from Hall's solitary writing endeavors. For more than three decades he was a steady contributor to journals such as the *Atlantic* and *Harper*'s. His own novels were more than just popular entertainment. He wrote in virtually every genre, and often dealt with important subjects of the time in an effective manner. Some of these well-respected novels that he wrote without a partner included *Kitchener's Mob, Lost Island, Doctor Dogbody's Leg, Under a Thatched Roof,* and *The Far Lands.* Despite the different genres he wrote, it was Polynesia that was his haven from the commercialism and rampant technological proliferation that was ravaging the modern world.

After writing about the death of one of his oldest South Seas friends in his book, *My Island Home: An Autobiography* (which was published posthumously), Hall would die of an apparent heart-attack at his home on July 5, 1951 at the age of 64. Upon his death, James Michener would write about him stating that Hall was the most beloved American who ever came to the tropics. "He had a gentle humor and abiding concern for people and a ready franc for anyone in need." Frisbie, who relied heavily on Hall's thoughts, praises, critiques, suggestions, perspectives, reasons, and friendship would have concurred with Michener's kind summation of the Woodshed Poet.

Before Frisbie passed away he had reached out to a friend named Peter Engle and his wife, Barbara in Honolulu, Hawaii, about taking in his daughters, especially Johnny, so that they could get an American education. The couple invited Johnny to live with them in Honolulu, and on April 22, 1950, she boarded a plane that would take her to Hawaii. Johnny recalled staring out the window at her sisters and noticed that none of them cried or even waved goodbye. They all knew that deep down inside themselves they would see each other again as it was her mother's dying wish to Frisbie that the girls would remain together. Johnny's sister, Elaine, was sent to New Zealand to live with Grace Sowerby and kept in touch through correspondence. Nga, the youngest sister, remained in Rarotonga with Mr. Willie and Marie Watson. The sister's separation would not last long as Johnny through innocent machinations, found a home in Hawaii for Nga with Lee and Sue-Mar Dawson. After picking up her sister at the airport, Johnny recalled proudly that they sat in silence in the back seat next to each other with their fingers intertwined. On November 28, 1952 Elaine joined her sisters in Hawaii to live with Mr. and Mrs. Pfaender and the trio were together once again.

Johnny would marry the popular radio and television host, Carl Hebenstreit, in 1956, and shortly after, the two moved to New Zealand. Although the couple would raise four children, they eventually divorced. Despite relationship issues and family obligations, Johnny remained devoted to her literary career. In 1959 she published her second book, *Frisbies of the South Seas* with Doubleday and Company, Inc. It was written as an autobiography much like her first book about how her father raised his children in Polynesia. The book had all the adventures, travels and reminiscence of her childhood, but without her father's meddling, yet supportive, hand. In 1965 the *Atlantic Monthly* published her reunion with her grandmother that took place on Pukapuka in the early 1960s.

EPILOGUE

Johnny would also publish numerous newspaper columns about life in the Pacific, and the Department of Education in Wellington, New Zealand, published many short stories about the children's experiences in the region. In the epilogue of the 2nd edition of her book, *Miss Ulysses of Puka-Puka*, which was published in 2016 at the age of 84, Johnny states that she continues to write and will do so until the final curtain falls on her earthly act and she sets off on her own voyage to *Po*. *Po* was a Polynesian underworld where the soul takes up residence and enjoys the various pleasures that was denied in the upper world.

As for the two *Tiare Taporo* captains, Viggo Rasmussen and Andy Thompson, the two would sail the schooner off and on until their dying day. Rasmussen left the boat in 1936 to become Resident Agent on Penrhyn Island where his wife and children lived. In 1945 ill health forced him to go to a better hospital on Rarotonga. Unfortunately, his health never truly recovered and after two years on Rarotonga he decided to sail the *Tiare Taporo* back to Penrhyn to spend his last days with his family. He would die in 1947 within the familiar sound of the mighty waves crashing upon the reef.

Andy Thompson on the other hand lived a very full, active life. He loved people and sometimes it would take him a week to cycle from Avarua to his home in Arorangi on the island of Rarotonga. As he visited his friends on the way home, he would have a yarn and a drink that most likely resulted in him having to stay the night. He would carry on throughout the week as he popped in and visited another friend until he eventually reached his house. Thompson would pass away on October 20, 1975 at the age of 90.

Suwarrow Island continues to have an eerie mystique

surrounding its islets. It is still considered the "treasure island" that fascinated Frisbie in the early 1940's and the stories of its ghosts and buried treasures can be heard throughout the region. The atoll has one of the best harbors in the Pacific Ocean and the reef encloses a large landlocked lagoon with pristine islets that are scattered around the rim. Because of its inaccessibility, it is known as one of the most perfect islands in the Cooks and a haven for the most intrepid adventurers especially those who dream of living alone on an idyllic tropical island.

One of those bold explorers was the New Zealander, Tom Neale who lived intermittently alone on the island for a total of fifteen years between 1952 and 1977. While working as a storekeeper and an advisor to local communities throughout Tahiti and the Cook Islands, Neale met Frisbie in Rarotonga. He was intrigued by the adventures that Frisbie told about his time living on Suwarrow. Frisbie's stories along with the proclivity of living in solitude inspired Neale to make the endeavor of living alone on the island. In 1952 at the age of 50 he made his first attempt by booking passage from a ship that he learned was passing close to the atoll. The ship dropped him with two cats and some provisions. He lasted two years then a back injury that he sustained while trying to rebuild the pier, or throwing an anchor from his boat, forced him back to civilization in Rarotonga. Neale's second stay on the atoll would last for three and half years from March 1960 to January 1964. This time his return to Rarotonga was mostly due to the fact that he became irritated with the many pearl divers who periodically arrived at his isolated world.

Neale wrote a memoir that recounts his time on Suwarrow through his second visit titled, *An Island to Oneself* which was reprinted in 1990 by Ox Bow Press. His autobiography detailed his self-sufficient life on the atoll and told how he fished, gardened, built things, domesticated animals and hosted a number of castaways and visitors. Neale became known as "The Hermit of Suwarrow." During an interview, he rebuked this nickname stating, "I'm not a hermit. Hermits don't like people but I do. I just live here because it suits me. I can do what I want, when I want, without being beholden to anyone. I'm free!" Obviously Frisbie's life was a major influence on him.

The book earned Neale the money to provide him with enough provisions for a longer stay on the atoll. He returned to Suwarrow in June 1967 and stayed until 1977 when he had to seek assistance for bad health from yachters who had visited the island. The yachters took Neale back to Rarotonga where he would die eight months later from stomach cancer at the age of 75. In 1978 Suwarrow was declared a national park of New Zealand. Every five years the government hires two caretakers to live on the atoll for six months and tend to the flora and fauna while residing in the huts that were left behind by Neale.

Pukapuka remains one of the most remote places on earth. Air Rarotonga has an irregular and unpredictable flight schedule to the atoll. If you do use the airline, you won't know when the return flight will be. If you are lucky, you might be able to catch a ship that calls into the island from time to time. About 400 Pukapukans live within a beautifully ordered and ancient *raui* system. This is a traditional system whereby access to a particular resource or area is forbidden for a given period. Additionally, this system allows the islanders to leave their normal village home and re-inhabit a customary village site in another part of the island to live, plant and fish. They also clean plantations, roads and paths. Then, after a certain amount of time, they return to the comforts of their modern home.

On the other hand, the remote atoll has not been immune to 21st century technology. Today there is an airstrip that makes access to the island a little easier. There are also homes that have running water, electricity and satellite TV. Even cellphone use is slowly gaining in popularity. I often wonder what Frisbie would think of his secluded atoll today. He definitely would have been skeptical about this progress and amused on how it would have changed the islander's lives. Clinical psychologist Amelia Borofsky, who grew up on the atoll recently stated, "The roosters still crow every morning, the men are playing toto (a game of throwing sticks) every afternoon on the main sandy road, and the kids splash in the lagoon as the sun sets over Yato Point." Frisbie would have been proud to see that Pukapukan culture would never completely capitulate to the encroachment of modern advancements and that traditions seem to remain unchanged now and, hopefully, for centuries to come.

Acknowledgments

There are many people that I wish to give my sincere gratitude since without their help the book would not have been possible. Thank you to Johnny Frisbie whose knowledge, encouragement and enthusiasm was instrumental with the completion of the project; Johnny's colleague and friend, Amelia Borofsky; Andrew Giambrone from *The Atlantic Monthly* who helped get me started with scans of RDF's articles; Jim Donald who shared with me information regarding the A.B. Donald Ltd. organization from his yacht, S.V. *Tiare Taporo III* while cruising around the Pacific Ocean; and Jean Mason, Manager, Cook Islands Library and Museum Society.

I would also like to thank for their help: Allison Haack, Library Assistant-Special Collections at the Burling Library Archive, Grinnell College; Vivienne at the James Norman Hall Home and Museum in Tahiti; staff in the Reading Room at the Huntington Library, staff from the Theosophical Library Center; and staff at the National Personnel Record Center of the U.S. National Archives, St. Louis.

I thank Mark Neal for his fine job of map-making and am grateful to Johnny Frisbie for granting permission to reproduce Frisbie family photos, to A. B. Donald Ltd. for permission to reproduce the photo of *Tiare Taporo* ,and to the James Norman Hall Home and Museum for photos of James Hall and

Charles Nordhoff. Other photos by author. Thanks also to Nancy J. Smith for the cover art.

I would also be remiss if I did not thank Pat Black for her eagle-eye proof reading; my wife Shannon, for inspiring me to keep going; and my daughter Devin, who questioned my topic subject. Sorry that it was not Harry Potter, but perhaps you will read it anyway.

ABOUT THE AUTHOR

Brandon Oswald studied archives and records management at the University of Dundee in Scotland. He is currently the Founder/Executive Director of the nonprofit organization, Island Culture Archival Support (ICAS) that is dedicated to providing voluntary archival assistance to cultural heritage organizations in the Pacific Islands. He has had several papers about cultural preservation in the Pacific Islands accepted at major conferences. Brandon lives in San Diego, California with his wife, Shannon, their daughter, Devin, three cats, and a dog named Steve.

For more about the author, visit www.brandonoswaldauthor.com.

BIBLIOGRAPHY

BOOKS:

DeLoughrey, Elizabeth. "White Fathers, Brown Daughters: The Frisbie Family Romance and the American Pacific." In *Literature and Racial Ambiguity*, edited by Teresa Hubel and Neil Brooks, 157-186. Amsterdam: Rodopi, 2002.

Frisbie, Johnny. *Miss Ulysses from Puka-Puka: The Autobiography of a South Sea Trader's Daughter*. New York: The Macmillan Company, 1948.

----. *Miss Ulysses from Puka-Puka: The Autobiography of a South Sea Trader's Daughter, 2nd ed.* Newport Beach: Dockside Sailing Press, 2016.

----. *The Frisbies of the South Seas*. Garden City: Double Day and Company Inc., 1959.

Frisbie, Robert Dean. *My Tahiti*. Boston: Little, Brown and Company, 1937.

----. *The Island of Desire: The Story of a South Sea Trader*. Garden City: Double Day, Doran and Company Inc., 1944.

BIBLIOGRAPHY

----. *Amaru*. Garden City: Doubleday, Doran and Co., Inc., 1945.

----. *The Book of Puka-Puka*. Honolulu: Mutual Publishing Company, 1957.

Gibson, Arrell Morgan. *Yankees in Paradise: The Pacific Basin Frontier*, Assisted By John S. Whitehead. Albuquerque: University of New Mexico Press, 1993.

Gilson, Richard. *The Cook Islands 1820-1950*. Wellington: Victoria University of Wellington, 1991.

Grove, Day A. and Carl Stroven, editors. *Best South Stories*. Honolulu: Mutual Publishing, 1964.

Hall, James Norman. *The Forgotten One and Other True Tales of the South Seas*. Honolulu: Mutual Publishing Company, 1987.

----. *My Island Home: An Autobiography*. Honolulu: Mutual Publishing, 2001.

Horwitz, Tony. Blue Latitudes: *Boldly Going Where Captain Cook Has Gone Before*. New York: Henry Holt and Company, 2002.

Meyers, Jeffrey. *Somerset Maugham: A Life*. New York: Alfred A. Knopf, 2004.

Moorehead, Alan. *The Fatal Impact: An Account of the Invasion of the South Pacific 1767-1840*. New York: Harper and Row Publishers, 1966.

Pieris, W.V.D. *The Manufacture of Copra in the Pacific Islands*. Noumea: South Pacific Commission, 1955.

Richards, T.L. and Stuart Gurr. *White Man, Brown Woman: The Life Story of a Trader in the South Seas*. Whitefish: Kessinger Publishing, LLC, 2010.

Salmond, Anne. *Aphrodite's Island: The European Discovery of Tahiti*. Berkeley: University of California Press, 2009.

Stevenson, Fanny. *The Cruise of the Janet Nichol among the South Seas Islands: A Diary by Mrs. Robert Louis Stevenson*, Edited by Roslyn Jolly. Sydney: University of New South Wales Press Ltd, 2004.

JOURNALS:

Clerk, Christian. "'That Isn't Really a Pig': Spirit Traditions in the Southern Cook Islands." *Oral Traditions* 5:2-3 (1990) : 316-333.

DeLoughrey, Elizabeth. "'The Whole is Made up of Many:' An Interview with Johnny Frisbie." *New Literatures Review* 38 (2002).

Frisbie, Robert Dean. "Fei-Hunting in Polynesia." *The Forum* (July 1924) : 92-99.

----. "Palmleaf Gambling Hells." *The Forum* (October 1925): 543-551.

----. "At Home in Puka-Puka: Life on an Atoll." *The Atlantic Monthly* (July 1928) : 1-12.

----. "Business as Usual." *The Atlantic Monthly* (October 1928) : 440-449.

----. "Adventures in a Puka-Puka Library." *The Atlantic Monthly* (February 1929) : 172-179.

----. "Puka-Puka Neighbors." *The Atlantic Monthly* (August 1929) : 186-195.

----. "South Sea Fairylands: A Kanaka Voyage." *The Atlantic Monthly* (August 1930) : 190-202.

----. "Full and By: A Kanaka Voyage." *The Atlantic Monthly* (September 1930) : 366-377.

----. "Davy Jones's Locker: The End of a Kanaka Voyage." *The Atlantic Monthly* (October 1930) : 493-503.

----. "Americans in the South Seas." *The American Mercury* (October 1931) : 154-160.

----. "Rum Row: Western." *The American Mercury* (May 1932) : 62-68.

----. "A Copra Island." *The Atlantic Monthly* (August 1932) : 192-200.

----. "Cinderella at Puka-Puka." *The Atlantic Monthly* (November 1934) : 610-615.

----. "Uninhabited Island." *The Atlantic Monthly* (November 1935) : 534-541.

----. "The Grandpapa of all the Fishes." *The Atlantic Monthly* (January 1936) : 40-52.

----. "Unconventional Journey: The Travels of Ropati." *The Atlantic Monthly* (December 1936) : 641-650.

----. "The Story of an Island: Marooned by Request." *The Atlantic Monthly* (August 1943) : 56-61.

----. "The Story of an Island: Marooned by Request." *The Atlantic Monthly* (September 1943) : 86-91.

----. "The Story of an Island: Marooned by Request." *The Atlantic Monthly* (October 1943) : 99-104.

----. "Economic Debauchery of Polynesians by Friendly Troops." *Pacific Islands Monthly* 14, no.6 (1944) : 19-20.

Kirkley, Evelyn A. "Starved and Treated Like Convicts: Images of Women in Point Loma Theosophy." *Journal of San Diego History* 43, no. 1 (1997) : 3-27.

Nordhoff, Charles. "An Island Memory." *The Atlantic Monthly* (September 1920) : 318-320.

----. "Rarotonga." *The Atlantic Monthly* (October 1920) : 456-463.

Porto, Angela. "Social Representations of Tuberculosis:

Stigma and Prejudice." *Revista de Saúde Pública* 41, Suppl. 1 (October 2007) : 43-49.

Ritchie, Jane and James Ritchie. "Polynesian Child Rearing: An Alternative Model." *Alternative Lifestyles* 5, no.3 (Spring 1983) : 126-141.

Williams, Lisa. "Celebrating a Famous Son." *Pacific Islands Monthly* 66, no.6 (1996) : 51.

WEB SOURCES:

"Albert Wendt." *Samoan Bios.* Accessed May 18, 2007. http://samoabios.com/albert-wendt/

"About Pukapuka: General Information About Pukapuka." *Pacific Islands Tourism Guide.* Accessed June 11, 2015. http://www.pacifictourism.travel/pacific-islands/about/cook-islands/pukapuka

"Bush Beer." *Cook Islands Travel Guide.* Accessed July 7, 2016..http://cookislands.southpacific.org/atiu/entertainment.html

"Capt. Andy Thompson." *Pacific Schooners.* Accessed February 19, 2015. http://pacificschooners.com/index.php/9-history/3-capt-andy-thompson

"Coastwatchers." *Olive-Drab.* Accessed May15, 2017. http://olive-drab.com/od_history_ww2_stories_1942coastwatchers.php

"Epeli Hau'ofa." Accessed May 18, 2017. http://epelihauofa.weebly.com/about.html

"Fiji Islands: Indo-Fijian History and Culture." *Jane's Fiji Home Page.* Accessed April 5, 2016. http://www.janesoceania.com/fiji_indo-fijian_history_culture/index.htm

"History of Tuberculosis and Its Prevalence in Newfoundland." *The Newfoundland and Labrador Heritage Website*. Accessed July 16, 2015. http://www.heritage.nf.ca/articles/society/tuberculosis-newfoundland.php

"James Norman Hall, The Man 1887-1951." Accessed September 19, 2016. http://www.jamesnormanhallhome.pf/jnhpage4.html

"John Williams South Seas Missionary." *Snippets from Tottenham's History*. Accessed September 12, 2016. http://tottenham-summerhillroad.com/

"Manihiki Island." *Jane's Cook Islands Home Page*. Accessed May 13, 2016. http://janeresture.com/manihiki/index.htm

"The New Books." Review of *Mr. Moonlight's Island*, by Robert Dean Frisbie. The Saturday Review, September 2, 1939 : 20. http:/unz.org/Pub/SaturdayRev-1939sep02-00020.

"Pacific Literature." *South Pacific Organizer*. Accessed May 18, 2007. http://www.southpacific.org/pacific/literature.html

"Pukapuka Island" *Jane's Cook Islands Home Page*. Accessed November 17, 2015. http://www.janeresture.com/pukapuka/

"Pukapuka: Land of Beautiful Girls." *The Cook Islands*. Accessed September 2, 2016. http://www.cookislands.org.uk/pukapuka.html#.WFAlMVUrJaR

"The Original *Tiare Taporo*." *Pacific Schooners* Accessed May 28, 2015. http://pacificschooners.com/index.php/9-history/2-the-original-tiare-taporo

"Religion in the Cook Islands. *The Cook Islands*." Accessed August 18, 2016. http://www.ck/religion.htm

"Robert Louis Stevenson." Accessed November 30, 2015. http://people.brandeis.edu/~teuber/stevensonbio.html

"Tetanus." *Better Health Channel*. Accessed March 4, 2016.

https://www.betterhealth.vic.gov.au/health/healthyliving/tetanus

"Tuberculosis in Europe and North America, 1800-1922." Contagion Historical Views Of Diseases and Epidemics. Accessed April 17, 2015. http://ocp.hul.harvard.edu/contagion/tuberculosis.htm

"The Universal Brotherhood and Theosophical Society." Accessed April 16, 2015. http://www.pointloma.edu/sites/default/files/filemanager/History_Political_Science/California_History_Tour.pdf

"World War I History." *History.com*. Accessed August 25, 2015. http://www.history.com/topics/world-war-i/world-war-i-history

Brown, Catherine Meredith. "Fiction Notes (8 Reviews)." Review of *Dawn Sails North*, by Robert Dean Frisbie. The Saturday Review, March 26, 1949 : 29-31. http://www.unz.org/Pub/SaturdayRev-1949mar26-00029

Gunson, Niel. "Williams, John (1796-1839)." Australian *Dictionary of Biography*. Accessed September 12, 2016. http://adb.anu.edu.au/biography/williams-john-2793

Kennedy, James Harrison. "A History of the City of Cleveland: Its Settlement, Rise and Progress 1796-1896." *Cleveland Memory Project*. Accessed April 21, 2016. http://www.clevelandmemory.org/ebooks/kennedy/

Lal, Brij V. "Fiji Islands: From Immigration to Emigration." *Migration Policy Institute*. Accessed April 5, 2016. http://www.migrationpolicy.org/article/fiji-islands-immigration-emigration

Mathieu, Benjamin. "Copra Farming." Accessed May 28, 2015. http://www.atolls-polynesie.ird.fr/resatoll/coprah/utilcopr/ukculcop.htm

Maurice, Arthur Bartlett. "Bon Voyage (5 Reviews)." Review of *The Book of Puka-Puka*, by Robert Dean Frisbie. The Bookman, December 1929. http://unz.org/Pub/Bookman-1929dec-x00163

Nordhoff, Charles. "Danger Island." Review of *The Book of Puka-Puka*, by Robert Dean Frisbie. The Saturday Review, December 7, 1929 : 510. http://unz.org/Pub/SaturdayRev-1929dec07-00510

Parsons, Bernard. "The Raja-Yoga Schools of Point Loma." Accessed April 16, 2015. http://www.theosociety.org/pasadena/sunrise/47-97-8/th-ktbp.htm

Potocnik, Natasa. "Robert Dean Frisbie: Writer of the South Seas: His Contribution to Pacific Literature." *Osaka University Knowledge Archive*. Last Modified October 3, 2011. http://ir.library.osakau.ac.jp/dspace/bitstream/11094/66631/riwl_005_119.pdf

Prodger, Phillip. "On High Seas: Jack London's Photography on the Cruise of the Snark." *Antiques*. Accessed April 27, 2015. http://www.themagazineantiques.com/articles/jack-london-snark/

Rakesh, Jim Donald. "A Potted History of the Original *Tiare Taporo*." *Tiare Taporo III* (blog), February 17, 2014 (6:11 a.m.). http://tiaretaporo3.blogspot.com/2014_02_01_archive.html

Roulston, Robert. "James Norman Hall: Past, Present, and Future." Accessed July 7, 2016. https://www.lib.uiowa.edu/scua/bai/roulston.htm

Other Sources:

Donald, Jim. "Re: A.B. Donald Ltd. Traders." Message to Brandon Oswald. 10 August 2015. E-mail.

Frisbie, Johnny. "Re: A Rarotonga Question." Message to Brandon Oswald. 24 July 2015. E-mail.

----. "Re: Quick Family Question." Message to Brandon Oswald. 29 July 2015. E-mail.

----. "Re: Photo Question." Message to Brandon Oswald. 1 May 2016. E-mail.

Hall, James Norman. Letter from Robert Dean Frisbie to James Norman Hall; Off Vancouver, B.C. *James Norman Hall Collection,* August 1931. Box 4, Folder 3, Grinnell College Libraries Special Collections, Burling Library Archives, Grinnell, Iowa.

Nordhoff, Charles. The Cook Islands. *Charles Bernard Nordhoff Papers, 1880-1950,* Box 1, Folder 7, The Huntington Library, Manuscript Department, San Marino, California.

----. Correspondence from Nordhoff. *Charles Bernard Nordhoff Papers, 1880-1950,* Box 3, Folder 17, The Huntington Library, Manuscript Department, San Marino, California.

----. Correspondence to Nordhoff and Family, 1940-1942. *Charles Bernard Nordhoff Papers, 1880-1950,* Box 4, Folder 4, The Huntington Library, Manuscript Department, San Marino, California.

THANK YOU FOR READING

If you enjoyed *Mr. Moonlight of the South Seas*, we invite you to leave a review online and share your thoughts and reactions online and with friends and family.

Publish Authority

www.ingramcontent.com/pod-product-compliance
Lightning Source LLC
Chambersburg PA
CBHW071414070526
44578CB00003B/575